"Hershfield and Aguirre have filled a notable gap in the field. Chapters walk the reader through how to understand intrusive thoughts and extreme emotions, and develop and implement effective tools for their management. The book is artfully crafted, engaging, and effectively conveys difficult-to-grasp concepts. This evidence-based text deserves to be on the shelves of affected individuals, as well as those who work to support them."

—**Eric A. Storch, PhD**, McIngvale presidential endowed chair and professor, and vice chair and head of psychology of the Menninger department of psychiatry and behavioral sciences at Baylor College of Medicine

"While many self-help books oversimplify concepts at the expense of honoring human complexity, Hershfield and Aguirre have written one that will appeal to people across diagnostic categories while providing valuable tools for skillful living. This book is the embodiment of the dialectical concepts it teaches, deftly exploring themes like tolerance and self-soothing, distraction and engagement, and, ultimately, acceptance and change. Even better, it's written with compassion and humor that make it a joy to read."

—**Amy Mariaskin, PhD**, founding director of the Nashville OCD & Anxiety Treatment Center, and author of *Thriving in Relationships When You Have OCD*

"Hershfield and Aguirre have masterfully merged their clinical knowledge (and humor) in this workbook to provide a practical, engaging, and evidenced-based guide for the many individuals I have seen who desperately need tools for BOTH facing their fears and coping effectively with emotions. Combining exposure and dialectical behavior therapy (DBT) in this manner is the first of its kind, and will be a reference I give my own clients for years to come."

—**Adam M. Reid, PhD**, co-owner and director of child and adolescent services at CBTeam

"Two best-in-class clinician educators have provided a clear, concise road map to gaining mastery over distressing thoughts and the intense emotions triggered by these thoughts. The concepts and practice of exposure and response prevention (ERP) and DBT are explained in a straightforward and practical way, making the integration of these powerful therapy tools accessible to all readers. I will be recommending this workbook enthusiastically to my patients and colleagues in clinical practice."

—**Michael Young, MD**, medical director of The Retreat at Sheppard Pratt, and associate program director of the University of Maryland/Sheppard Pratt psychiatry residency program

"Jon Hershfield and Blaise Aguirre are a dynamic duo. Their combined expertise in cognitive behavioral therapy (CBT) and DBT fills this workbook with clear explanations, practical tips, and numerous exercises to help one navigate the hard work of managing unwanted thoughts and intense emotions. The concepts and skills discussed are applicable to a wide audience, no matter where you are on your journey."

—**Maria Fraire, PhD**, program director of the OCD Institute for Children and Adolescents at McLean Hospital, and instructor in psychology at Harvard Medical School

"Starting exposure therapy to ride through unwanted thoughts is a tremendously difficult task. When we face what we avoid, we often experience strong waves of emotions. In this book, the authors did an excellent job incorporating two core therapy modalities—ERP and DBT, showing readers that big emotions can be understood and coped with (DBT), and intrusive thoughts are best managed when observed and experienced (ERP)."

—**P. Esra Guvenek-Cokol, MD**, medical director of McLean Hospital Child and Adolescent OCD Institute (OCDI Jr); McLean Hospital Support, Treatment, and Resilience Program (STAR)

"It is refreshing to see something finally addressed in this book that has bugged a lot of therapists in the last —can we get ERP and DBT to be able to work together for the treatment of obsessive-compulsive disorder (OCD)? Focusing on the common goal that they both have—to end the suffering caused by intense emotional experiences—Jon and Blaise walk us through the synergy that is made utilizing principles from both camps to show us how treatment can be effectively rendered."

—**Patrick B. McGrath, PhD**, chief clinical officer of NOCD, and fellow of the Association for Behavioral and Cognitive Therapies IOCDF Scientific and Clinical Advisory Board

Unwanted Thoughts & Intense Emotions Workbook

CBT & DBT Skills to Break the Cycle of

Intrusive Thoughts & Emotional Overwhelm

Jon Hershfield, MFT • Blaise Aguirre, MD

New Harbinger Publications, Inc.

Publisher's Note

This publication is designed to provide accurate and authoritative information in regard to the subject matter covered. It is sold with the understanding that the publisher is not engaged in rendering psychological, financial, legal, or other professional services. If expert assistance or counseling is needed, the services of a competent professional should be sought.

NEW HARBINGER PUBLICATIONS is a registered trademark of New Harbinger Publications, Inc.

New Harbinger Publications is an employee-owned company.

Cover design by Sara Christian

Acquired by Jess O'Brien

Edited by Cynthia Nixon

Library of Congress Cataloging-in-Publication Data on file

Printed in the United States of America

26   25   24

10   9   8   7   6   5   4   3

Contents

Foreword   v

About the Authors   vii

About This Book   ix

Part One:
Treating Your Unwanted Thoughts and Intense Emotions

Chapter 1   Understanding Unwanted Thoughts   3

Chapter 2   Understanding Difficult Emotions   17

Chapter 3   The Fundamentals of CBT and ERP for Unwanted Thoughts   25

Chapter 4   The Fundamentals of DBT for Intense Emotions   47

Chapter 5   ERP and DBT Together   71

Part Two:
Effective Skills for Complex Experiences

Chapter 6   Coping vs. Compulsing   81

Chapter 7   Engaging Your Thoughts and Emotions Skillfully vs. Escalating Your Distress   91

Chapter 8   Accepting Unwanted Thoughts vs. Believing Untruths   97

Chapter 9   Distracting from Unwise Behaviors vs. Avoiding the Hard Things   105

Chapter 10   Addressing Shame vs. Being Hijacked by Shame   111

Chapter 11   Reflecting Mindfully vs. Self-Criticism   119

Chapter 12   Self-Compassion vs. Making Excuses   129

Part Three:
Putting the Tools to Use

Chapter 13   Choose Your Own Mental Health Plan of Action   135

Chapter 14   The Power of Validation   147

Chapter 15   Everything in One Place   153

               For Further Reading   157

Foreword

This topic is very close to my heart. I have been working with people with OCD and intense emotional distress for almost three decades and have seen, firsthand, the tremendous challenges that these issues can bring. The authors of this book courageously take on this issue–focusing on helping people struggling with emotional overwhelm and intrusive thoughts.

For context, most of my training in psychology and OCD has been through working with OCD sufferers that failed traditional outpatient treatment and sought intensive OCD treatment (such as residential OCD treatment). I have been involved in treating over 1000 patients. I am also a co-director of psychology training and the director of the CBT-focused partial hospital at McLean Hospital. It is through these two different roles that I met the authors, Jon and Blaise; I met Jon through my OCD work and Blaise through my work at McLean. It is not often that two exceptional therapists with very different specialties get together and write such a book–Jon as an OCD therapist and Blaise as a DBT therapist. They are amazing educators and have collectively written over twenty books. Together they are fun and funky, the quintessential "odd" couple! They both care deeply about their patients, have a wonderful sense of humor, and work collaboratively with their clients; this compassionate, caring, and fun tone is clear throughout this book. I have had the great pleasure to present at conferences with both of them and they are wonderful teachers in their respective fields. Now they have combined their unique skill sets, in working with OCD patients and in providing DBT therapy, through this workbook.

In my humble opinion, one of the more challenging issues that people take on in life is to sincerely and absolutely engage in treatment. We do, in fact, have very effective treatment for OCD and a meaningful way of helping people manage overwhelming emotions, but how on Earth do you really get people to engage and do the challenging work that is needed?

I am reminded of a young patient that came to my program a while back—let's call her Amy. She struggled with severe OCD and felt completely overwhelmed by her painful emotions. Her family brought her to me and she did not want to enter treatment. Numerous therapists told Amy that her OCD was too severe to be treated and her emotional challenges were too much to handle. For some reason, after our first meeting, she agreed to engage in treatment and stay at the residential program that I was directing at the time. She did wonderfully and had her OCD under control in two months and was ready to leave. In fact, today she is a therapist herself and we have presented a few times together on her journey through treatment. I was never really clear why she did decide to do the hard work and truly engage in treatment after that first meeting. Then at one of our presentations so many years later, she revealed that she always remembered the feeling when someone could talk to her about her struggles in a way that she understood. This feeling led her to feel hopeful for the first time in her life that she might actually get better. Truly validating where she was at the time, recognizing her emotional turmoil, and educating her about the effective treatment available to her gave her enough hope to engage in treatment. This workbook, which you hopefully will read and engage in–after reading my foreword, of course–sincerely and thoughtfully provides the framework for you to truly understand and begin the hard work of overcoming unwanted thoughts and managing emotional turmoil, just as Amy did. I wish both Amy and I had access to a book like this long ago–I think it would have made the work so much easier.

Not all have such a strong positive response to treatment as Amy did, and many have had to shift course to work on emotional challenges first and then OCD and related challenges, or vice versa. This book provides a sound way to navigate this journey, emphasizing different ways you can simultaneously work through these complex symptoms.

The book is accessible and clear. Jon and Blaise use lots of examples and provide wonderful scenarios of how people have used the skills they present in this book and how their work could relate to you. Given my experience in treating people with these challenges, I can attest that they follow the evidence and stay true to the most effective treatment approaches, adding their rich clinical experience and compassion. The book is divided into three parts: Part I provides education to lay the foundation, Part II provides examples and details the ways to take on the challenges, and Part III provides roadmaps for you to begin the challenging work on your own.

A workbook like this can be so powerful in teaching how to implement the work. In a residential OCD program that I founded over two decades ago, we usually gave a workbook to every counselor that worked with us. We learned that this was an especially effective way of teaching people about OCD treatment, in addition to all the other things we did during the training of our staff. We also gave a copy of a recent workbook to each patient that attended our program to help with learning and to enhance the efficacy of the treatment. This book, for me, is now on top of the list of books to give to staff and clients alike, as it provides a sound resource of ways to do the OCD work and handle emotional turmoil.

I thoroughly enjoyed reading this book and working through it–I hope you will too. I think the "odd" couple, Jon and Blaise, with their powerful combination of skills and expert knowledge, have created something unique here.

—Thröstur Björgvinsson, PhD, ABPP,
  director of the Behavioral Health Partial Hospital
  Program at McLean Hospital and associate professor
  of psychology in the Department of Psychiatry at
  Harvard Medical School

About the Authors

About Jon

I became a specialist in obsessive-compulsive disorder (OCD) by working almost exclusively with people who have OCD throughout my career. Like many master's-level clinicians, I went straight from graduate school to essentially "being a therapist," missing out on the kind of formal training programs doctorate-level clinicians often go through. I compensated for this by reading as much as I could about OCD and devouring as much OCD-related content as I could from educational conferences. I listened closely to my mentors and drew from my own experience with the disorder to come to the easy conclusion that cognitive behavioral therapy (CBT) with exposure and response prevention (ERP) is the most effective treatment for OCD and similar disorders.

But no one taught me more about OCD than my clients. As I learned from these brave people whose minds seemed out to get them, I started to notice that some had more difficulty than others with getting well. They didn't fail to understand the concepts or even to implement them; the process of getting better just seemed to be its own trigger. Every time a little progress would get made, a wall of shame or some other kind of emotional intensity would reliably flood the room like a tsunami. It would push the OCD treatment aside and insist that this person doesn't deserve to be happy, to be still, to be loved, or, even in some cases, to be alive! This tsunami would sometimes have a name, like "borderline personality disorder," but it often managed to evade *Diagnostic and Statistical Manual of Mental Disorders* criteria. I became increasingly frustrated that mindfulness, or simply accepting unwanted thoughts and emotions, was not sufficient to keep my clients meaningfully engaged in the work.

As director of the Center for OCD and Anxiety at Sheppard Pratt in Baltimore, I noticed that many of those seeking our residential services for OCD were also struggling with emotion regulation. Unwanted thoughts brought on more than just anxiety or disgust, but sometimes also hopelessness, despair, anger, and self-hatred. While I served as witness to the courageous but battle-worn patients who came for this high level of treatment, my hypothesis was confirmed. People are not the net sum of their diagnoses. People almost universally have difficulty forming a stable and loving relationship between their thoughts and their emotions, their fears and their distress. My hope is that this book helps to heal that relationship.

About Blaise

I went to medical school to become a psychiatrist and, upon doing so, found myself drawn to people presenting with the most complex conditions, such as borderline personality disorder (BPD). People with BPD were somewhat of an enigma to me: on the one hand, they were some of the most talented and introspective individuals I had ever met; on the other, they seemed to suffer more than many of my other patients, at times to the point where they considered suicide to be the only way out.

In my training, I was taught that BPD was an almost impossible disorder to treat and that most of the approaches to do so used traditional talk therapies. I was trained in these kinds of therapies; however, even though my patients seemed to feel understood by them, they didn't get all that much better from them, at least not in my hands. It was when I got to McLean Hospital in Belmont, Massachusetts, in 2000 that I first heard about a treatment known as dialectical behavior therapy (DBT), which combined the talk therapies I was well versed in with something called behavior therapy—an approach I knew very little about that included the practice of mindfulness, something I knew even less about.

I was formally trained in DBT in 2007 and have not looked back since. Later that same year, I opened, with colleagues, the 3East treatment center at McLean. 3East is unique in that it focuses solely on the use of DBT to treat adolescents and young adults who struggle with regulating their emotions. Although the treatment is not a cure-all, time and again, I've seen many young patients and their families finally find a way out of their suffering. It was their progress more than anything else that convinced me of the efficacy of this new approach, and since we opened, we have treated nearly four thousand complicated young people with high-risk behaviors. Today, I regularly get invitations to their families' graduations, engagements, weddings, christenings, and, most recently, a bris.

Despite our success, I wasn't completely content. Yes, we're helping many people, yet many still struggle. We've found that comorbid post-traumatic stress disorder (PTSD), eating disorders, substance use disorders, and OCD complicate or impede a speedy recovery.

My hope is that this book will provide ideas—some old and some new—to address these complications and that readers will find a way out of the struggle by regularly practicing the skills provided herein in an effortful and informed journey toward recovery.

About This Book

In the OCD treatment community, we understand one thing really, really well: exposure works. Exposure to things that make us feel uncertain, when paired with the absence of compulsions, forces the brain to recalculate its position on what we can and cannot tolerate. Reasonable people can debate over style and strategy in exposure-based treatment, but that's a question of how to get there, not a question of where to go. The problem is, when we do get there, it's often unclear what we're supposed to do. We know what not to do (which is anything that might function as avoidance or suppression of the exposure), but when in the midst of exposure to our fears, most people's answer to the question of what to do is often just the equivalent of *Well, suffer.*

If you have had any experience with exposure-based treatment, you may have been told to "sit" with your discomfort. For some, this is just a matter of waiting out the unpleasant thoughts and emotions. But for others, the experience of sitting with some thoughts and feelings creates changes in the brain that are not manageable. Terror, trauma, self-loathing, anger, suicidal thoughts (and sometimes actions), and overall psychic chaos arise. Reliable and accessible tools are needed to address these feelings that are part of the conditioned response to triggering thoughts. If the instruction is simply to put up with it, the "it" changes. For the person with relentlessly painful emotions, the learning sought in exposure cannot take place. The brain is too busy with the new project of psychological arson and evisceration to learn anything of value. The takeaway from the experience is not *I did a hard thing and survived,* but *I did something foolish because I am a failure.*

In the DBT treatment community, we also understand one thing really, really well: emotion regulation strategies work. *Emotion regulation* is a term used to describe the ability to effectively manage and respond to an emotional experience. Most of us use emotion regulation strategies to cope with difficult moments throughout the course of each day in order to effectively deal with the demands of whatever situation we're in. But here's the thing: some of these strategies are healthy and adaptive, and some are not. For instance, being upset and going for a walk to calm down will do us no harm. Going for a walk can help us focus on something else and allow for time to help diffuse the situation. On the other hand, there are emotion regulation strategies that work but are harmful and maladaptive. Behaviors like substance use and self-injury can be effective in the short run only to lead to more intense emotions and suffering in the long run.

The problem is that these short-term maladaptive solutions work very quickly, so some people feel that substituting them for things that might not work, or at least might not work as well, is not worth the risk. You may have found that your maladaptive strategies work pretty well against unwanted intense emotions you're only too familiar with, so doing something different, like learning new emotion regulation coping strategies, can seem like a lot of work. It certainly can be. The work involved in developing emotion regulation skills includes being able to stay in an emotion long enough to learn that it is bearable and then learn how to deal with it more adaptively. Sitting with a strong emotion can lead to feelings of shame, guilt, self-loathing, enduring pain, and, when very extreme, urges to self-injure and thoughts of suicide. A fundamental principle of brain functioning is that the brain in distress cannot easily learn new material, such as new coping skills. A person has to regulate before they can reflect. You have to see what you're really dealing with *clearly* in order to identify how to address it effectively.

So, what does a person do when plagued with unshakable thoughts and unbearable emotions at the same time? There are ample self-help resources that address unwanted thoughts (and disorders like OCD where they are most prevalent) and there are a number of books that address difficult emotions (and disorders like BPD), but we hope this book will stand out as an essential bridge between these two worlds. Exclusive focus on confronting fears and anxiety leaves many feeling overwhelmed and inadequate. Exclusive focus on calming down leaves many feeling weak and imprisoned by fear. This book is designed to help you navigate those especially sticky thoughts that send you into a tailspin and those especially painful emotions that keep you trapped in your negative stories.

At the core of this book lies the concept that our emotional response to thoughts and our intellectual response to emotions both arise from *conditions*. In other words, we learn that when we have one kind of thought, it makes us feel one kind of way, and when we have one kind of feeling, it makes us think one kind of thing. We learn these conditions, and then they become hardwired over time by repeatedly responding to them with behaviors that keep them bound together. For example, if you have a thought about getting sick, you may feel fear, and then you might avoid the thing that made you think about getting sick, and that "sick = fear" conditioning sticks reliably. If you feel shame and you think *I am bad* and then criticize yourself harshly, then, again, this conditioning of the emotion to the thought sticks reliably. But if we can learn to relate to these thought-emotion and emotion-thought pairs differently by changing our behavior, we can liberate ourselves from repeating the same patterns over and over. ERP and DBT are two behavioral strategies that we will invite you to explore in this book.

In part one, we offer a rundown of the main targets of this book: thoughts and feelings. What are they really? Why do we take them so seriously? How do they lead to behaviors, and how do those behaviors inform additional thoughts and feelings? We also explain the core tenets of ERP and DBT and why we think they complement rather than oppose each other.

In part two, we look at some of the common challenges people face when trying to navigate their unwanted thoughts and difficult emotions at the same time. For example, where should we draw the line between calming ourselves down and compulsively running away from hard feelings? When does exposing ourselves to what scares us turn into simply getting ourselves overwhelmed without benefit?

How are we to deal with complex emotions like shame and anger that may arise when trying to grapple with unwanted thoughts? How can we tell when we're being self-compassionate as opposed to avoiding taking responsibility for our actions? These and other thorny spots in the treatment of unwanted thoughts and intense emotions will be examined. We will also ask you to reflect on these types of challenges and think about the skills you would use when any of them arise.

Part three of this book offers a series of "choose your own adventure"–style templates that represent common ways people struggle with unwanted thoughts and difficult emotions. We've designed a format that will allow you to identify which CBT and DBT tools would benefit you as you create your personalized treatment approach.

PART ONE

Treating Your Unwanted Thoughts and Intense Emotions

Get ready for a complete and total assault on your mind and body—the densest, most complicated, and infuriating workbook you will ever encounter, guaranteed to leave you more confused and less capable. No, wait, sorry, that's another book we're working on for another publisher.

What lies ahead in the next few chapters may look complex, but it's relatively straightforward: thoughts, feelings, and two treatment strategies that can help you effectively navigate them. There will be several instances where we encourage you to write things down or complete exercises by filling out worksheets. These are designed to help you lock in some of the concepts, but they are absolutely voluntary (and we're not watching, anyway).

If you came to this book because of difficulties with unwanted thoughts, we still recommend you read the chapters on emotions and how to treat them. If you came to this book primarily because of difficulty tolerating intense emotions, we still recommend you read the chapters on unwanted thoughts and how to navigate them as well. You have probably already come to the same conclusion we did when we thought of writing this book: thoughts and emotions are interconnected, so their treatments should be as well. Let's take a look, shall we?

CHAPTER 1

Understanding Unwanted Thoughts

When considering what unwanted thoughts really are, we often fail to remember one simple concept: they are normal events. Brains produce unwanted thoughts. Problems arise when certain thoughts become conditioned to essentially pull along certain feelings with them. In other words, the brain forms associations that make sense over time. If an emotion seems useful (as when fear leads to avoiding something dangerous), it will keep popping up whenever the brain is cued to protect you. The word "car" might not inspire any particular emotion in you, but if you had recently been in a car accident, the situation could be different—the word "car" might bring on memories of being in danger and feeling afraid. And remembering that could make you feel like you're somehow in danger right now, reading this book. Let's try an exercise to demonstrate how thoughts and feelings are conditioned together.

Take a moment to recall the last time someone gave you a compliment or a gift, then write it down here:

_____

How do you feel right now while reflecting on that?

_____

Interesting, isn't it? You didn't get another gift just now, but in a way, it may feel as if you did. Now consider this: think of the last time you made a mistake and someone noticed. Bring up the memory of having erred and someone having commented critically on it, then write it down here:

_____

Well? How do you feel?

_____

It's fascinating, right? Thoughts become conditioned to pull feelings up to the forefront of the mind based on our experiences. It's inescapable. We think of something pleasing, and we feel good; we think of something displeasing, and we feel bad. The thoughts themselves are as empty as words on a piece of paper (as we will discuss shortly), but they can bring on such intense emotional experiences that it appears as if thoughts have a lot of power over us. The way we respond to these emotions in our behavior (often in an attempt to get the unpleasant ones to leave and the pleasant ones to stay) leads to new experiences, and these experiences bring on new thoughts and new conditioned feelings along with them. It can be dizzying—thoughts leading to feelings leading to more thoughts and feelings! This is why you picked up this workbook, so you could learn a multilateral approach for navigating this frustrating two-pronged experience.

What Is a Thought?

Try this: see if you can define the word "thought" without using the word "thinking" or just substituting the word for something fancy like "cognition." It's very difficult. You might describe thoughts as "things you say to yourself," and that's a pretty good definition, but it fails to capture those thoughts that feel alien or disconnected from your typical self-talk.

Ironically, thoughts guide almost everything we do, yet we don't even know what they are. The closest definition we can "think" of is one that applies to everything we notice: an object of consciousness. Not very satisfying, we know, but it does explain a lot. A thought is an object in the sense that it's something you can observe, and the place you are observing it is in your consciousness. Before you finish this sentence, you will have a thought about what's coming at the end of it. If we ask you to picture a cat right now, a cat object will arise in your consciousness and you will know that you are experiencing it. For most, this experience will be neutral, but other thoughts might orbit this image like moons, saying things like "I like cats" or "I don't like cats." Depending on how you are conditioned to respond to these judgment types of thoughts, an emotional or physical response might arise in you next.

Some thoughts trigger such profound emotional responses that we view them as inherently harmful. Imagine watching a scary movie on TV and blaming the television set for the distress it caused! The movie is just lights and sounds, but our conditioning leads some lights and sounds to make us feel threatened, angered, or sad. Different kinds of thoughts may arise in different ways so that it can almost feel impossible to be objective about them. One helpful way to understand this is recognizing the difference between thoughts that intrude like junk mail in your inbox (a normal but undesired event) versus thoughts that make sense to you (even though they may be unhelpful).

Ego-Dystonic Thoughts

As you read these words right now, you're doing so from the perspective of a "self"—a kind of story about who you are. You have a personal narrative or identity of some kind made up of countless parts beyond your name. Your religious and moral beliefs, your cultural context, your memories of past acts and fantasies about future acts all intertwine to form a *you* that is sometimes called the "ego."

An *ego-dystonic thought* is one that does not match up with your understood sense of self. In other words, it seems odd to you that this is the thought going through your head. This can be because the thought itself is out of line with your beliefs (like a violent thought toward someone you'd never wish to harm), out of line with what you view as reasonable (like thinking you'll get a disease because a strand of your hair touched something dirty), or out of line with what you remember (a thought that suggests you didn't turn off the stove when you remember doing it). Part of what triggers unwanted emotions is this sense that the thoughts really don't belong in your head!

Take a moment to consider ego-dystonic thoughts that press your buttons and write a few of them down here. Later in the book when we explore treatment strategies, you can use these thoughts as examples.

_____

_____

_____

_____

Ego-Syntonic Thoughts

Thoughts that *do* make sense to you and fit into your worldview are called *ego-syntonic thoughts*. Content-wise, they have the same range as ego-dystonic thoughts. Thinking the stove is on when you actually know the stove is on would be an ego-syntonic thought. Disturbing thoughts, such as a thought about hurting someone, can be ego-syntonic if you genuinely wish to cause someone pain. Even bizarre thoughts, such as *Someone is spying on me through my coffee cup*, can be ego-syntonic if the thinker has a condition that causes them to genuinely believe this.

Thoughts called "obsessions" (characteristic of OCD) are typically ego-dystonic. The thinker does not enjoy the thoughts, nor do they seem consistent with the thinker's general understanding of how the world is supposed to work. Trying to get rid of these thoughts, as if they were contaminants of the mind, is how people with OCD and related disorders find themselves doing compulsions.

Trickier territory to navigate is when a thought is both dystonic and syntonic throughout the day or at the same time. For example, a person could be distressed by unwanted intrusive thoughts of self-harm and desperately want certainty that they would never act on these ego-dystonic thoughts. But that same person may be so overwhelmed emotionally by the relentless and graphic nature of these thoughts, they could simultaneously have thoughts of genuinely wishing to harm themselves as a form of relief from their distress.

Some ego-syntonic thoughts can bring along as much or more emotional anguish as ego-dystonic thoughts. If you feel someone has wronged you, broken your rules, or made your life more difficult in some way, you may experience thoughts of resentment, even for people you care about and who care about you. If you struggle with your own sense of worth and have thoughts of not being good enough or of being a failure, you might experience all manner of dreadful negative commentary in your head, and you mean it all at the time! How you feel in the moment makes a tremendous difference in how you relate to these thoughts. Consider the difference between thinking *I hate myself* while experiencing tremendous guilt over something you did versus having that same thought pop into your head because you accidentally gave yourself a paper cut. Both experiences may be overwhelming, but the former probably has a longer-lasting sting and a few more thoughts and feelings trailing it.

Take a moment to write down some of the ego-syntonic thoughts you have that cause you distress. Remember, these are thoughts you believe when they arise and make sense to you in the moment you have them, but they still bother you and cause you to experience difficult emotions.

_____

_____

_____

_____

_____

_____

_____

POP QUIZ!

Take a look at this list and see if you can distinguish between the ego-syntonic and the ego-dystonic thoughts:

- *There's too much sweetener in this coffee.*

- *What if I just snapped and attacked the dog for no reason?*

- *I should hurt myself because it will distract me from my guilt.*

- *I don't think gray socks go with brown shoes.*

- *I'm going to steal something from this store for no reason even though I don't want to!*

- *That wasn't a speed bump; I just hit a pedestrian and somehow didn't realize it until just now.*

- *I'm disappointed I didn't get a better grade on that test.*

If you found this quiz a bit confusing, good! It suggests you're paying attention. What makes a thought syntonic or dystonic may not always be clear-cut because, depending on the context, even our most unpleasant thoughts can seem completely in line with our feelings. Similarly, many thoughts that seem to line up with our values can also come in the form of "what ifs" and might be deceptively ego-dystonic too.

Conditions That Involve Unwanted Thoughts

It is not necessary for you to have a psychiatric diagnosis to benefit from a book on how to handle upsetting thoughts and emotions. However, there are several conditions in which people have such difficulty letting go of their unwanted thoughts and the feelings that come with them that it can truly impair functioning. As we will explore later, how we respond to our thoughts when they arise largely affects how we feel about them, and how we feel about them in turn has an effect on how they appear when they show up again.

Below is a list of common mental health diagnoses that typically involve a struggle with unwanted thoughts that trigger unpleasant feelings and lead to unhelpful behaviors that can keep you feeling trapped. You may identify with one, all, or none of these. But it may be helpful to observe how each of these conditions follows a similar pattern. There is an unwanted thought, an unpleasant emotional reaction, and an unhelpful behavior or series of behaviors aimed at avoiding both. We'll explain why avoidance doesn't help in the chapters ahead.

Obsessive-Compulsive Disorder

OCD is characterized by *obsessions* (unwanted intrusive thoughts, images, or urges) and *compulsions* (mental or physical responses to the obsessions). Obsessive content can come in an unlimited number of forms, but more common concerns for those with OCD relate to contamination, harm, symmetry/exactness, or taboo/unacceptable thoughts. Compulsions are strategies for reducing distress associated with these unwanted thoughts, usually in the form of trying to eliminate doubt or uncertainty about the thoughts. Common examples include excessive handwashing or cleaning, checking behaviors, organizing or evening things up, and a wide variety of mental rituals. While everyone has unwanted thoughts and engages in rituals, people with OCD get stuck in such a loop trying to make their thoughts and distress go away that it grossly impairs functioning.

Generalized Anxiety Disorder

Much like OCD, generalized anxiety disorder (GAD) involves unwanted thoughts and unhelpful responses. Here, though, the thoughts tend to be a bit closer to home, focused on work, finances, health, and relationships. Ineffective responses to these intrusive thoughts might include avoidance, reassurance seeking, and, most of all, excessive worrying and ruminating.

Body Dysmorphic Disorder

Body dysmorphic disorder (BDD) involves unwanted intrusive thoughts about one's appearance. While most of us have things we may not like about our bodies, people with BDD may focus very intensely on one aspect of their appearance and view it as deformed, disgusting, or shamefully unattractive. This can be completely disconnected from what others see or a gross magnification of a slight difference. Compulsions may include avoidance, reassurance seeking, camouflaging, skin picking, and, in extreme cases, having surgical procedures to change the triggering body part.

Social Anxiety Disorder

Social anxiety disorder (SAD) or social phobia is characterized by unwanted intrusive thoughts about negative evaluation from others. People who struggle with this condition are excessively concerned with how others view them and become distressed and overwhelmed in social situations. Social anxiety can be experienced in intimate one-on-one interactions, small groups, or large crowds. Common compulsions include avoidance of social situations, reassurance seeking, rumination (replaying conversations), mental rehearsal (overpreparing for social interactions), and other attempts to try to control what others may be thinking.

Illness Anxiety Disorder

Formerly called hypochondriasis, illness anxiety disorder (IAD) involves unwanted intrusive thoughts about one's health. People who struggle with this condition can develop a singular focus on the fear of getting a particular disease or a more abstract fear of having "something wrong" with them medically. Common compulsions involve excessive online research and reassurance seeking, avoidance of people and places they associate with getting sick, and a variety of mental rituals. Excessive visits to doctors for medical tests are also very common, though some may excessively avoid doctors out of fear of receiving bad news.

Panic Disorder with Agoraphobia

Panic attacks are physiological events characterized by high anxiety, shortness of breath, chest tightness, dizziness, and a co-occurring fear of dying. They can occur in response to something triggering, such as a feeling of being trapped, they can be a reaction to certain medications or recreational drugs, or they can occur spontaneously without warning. Agoraphobia is a fear of being out of the house. Many people who have experienced panic attacks worry that an attack may occur again and will compulsively avoid situations where this could be difficult. For example, someone with this condition may avoid air travel because of not being able to leave if a panic attack occurs mid-flight.

Specific Phobias

Much like OCD, specific phobias involve intrusive thoughts, but with a singular focus on one target of fear, like dogs, heights, or vomiting. These intrusive thoughts may be responded to with any number of compulsions besides avoidance, such as reassurance seeking, superstitious rituals, and mental rituals.

Post-Traumatic Stress Disorder

Unlike OCD, PTSD involves unwanted intrusive thoughts about real traumatic events alongside the fear that these events might occur again. In addition to several other symptoms (such as nightmares and flashbacks), people with PTSD may develop a variety of rituals that look very similar to compulsions in OCD. There is also often a significant amount of avoidance of things that may trigger traumatic memories, and this avoidance can at times be so significant that it impairs functioning in much the same way that severe OCD can.

Borderline Personality Disorder

One might initially think a personality disorder is very different from the mental health conditions listed above, but BPD is also characterized by difficulty coping with unwanted thoughts and the feelings they elicit. In particular, people with BPD often struggle with unwanted thoughts about trust and relationships, being rejected or abandoned, being unlovable, being harmed by others, or harming oneself. We will explore this condition in more detail ahead when we take a closer look at emotions, but we wanted to plant a flag here to note how people show up in this world in so many ways and yet often face very similar struggles to cope with thoughts and feelings.

Though these are all different disorders, what they have in common is the same push and pull that likely led you to this workbook. It can be so hard to simply view thoughts as "objects of consciousness" when they seem to be dragging along such intense emotions that any "reasonable" person would want to escape. Now let's take a look at the different types of thoughts that have a particular tendency to elicit strong emotional reactions.

Types of Triggering Thoughts

Triggering thoughts, as defined in this book, can be ego-dystonic or ego-syntonic. In the pages ahead, we'll demonstrate how this informs most therapeutic approaches to these thoughts and the painful emotions that come with them. In addition to the syntonic/dystonic nature of thoughts, we are conditioned to respond to some types of thoughts as especially distressing.

Taboo or Unacceptable Thoughts

Taboo thoughts fall outside of your beliefs about cultural norms. One person's taboo thoughts can be another person's vanilla thoughts and vice versa. Taboo thoughts are basically those that society or religion has told us are naughty, inappropriate, or forbidden. They are not inherently bad (again, thoughts are just mental objects), but they may be perceived that way. Some people can recognize their taboo thoughts and shrug them off, even enjoy them, while others may become aware of the same thoughts and feel tremendous guilt, shame, or fear.

Unacceptable thoughts more generally tend to involve themes of behaving harmfully or inappropriately. For those with OCD, unwanted (dystonic) sexual or violent thoughts are common obsessions. Other common unacceptable thoughts involve ideas of social unacceptability, such as thoughts about a tragic death being funny—in other words, thoughts that would be met with disapproval if spoken aloud. Those who struggle with religious scrupulosity (obsessions about one's faith) may find themselves burdened by unacceptable thoughts that go against their religious tenets. Similarly, those with moral scrupulosity may feel distressed by thoughts that arise and appear to contradict their own values.

Further, some people struggle with thoughts they have simply deemed unacceptable, though there's nothing inherently bad about them. For example, you may love and feel attracted to your partner but have a thought about them being unattractive. While it is completely normal to notice when someone you usually find attractive is not looking their best, someone who is committed to the belief that they should always find their partner attractive is going to label this thought "unacceptable" and be distressed by its presence.

Thoughts in this category often bring up a lot of guilt (feeling as if you did something wrong) or shame (feeling as if you are an inherently bad or immoral person). These feelings can be extraordinarily intense and can lead to depression and despair that can escalate into self-hatred, urges to isolate, and even self-harm. It cannot be stated enough that these "unacceptable" thoughts are actually very common and, truth be told, totally acceptable as thoughts. You may be conditioned to think that just hearing words in your head that describe a terrible deed, some sick or twisted behavior that offends you, is in and of itself a bad act (this is sometimes referred to as "thought-action fusion"). But a thought is not an act any more than a picture of a sandwich is a satisfying lunch.

Take a moment to jot down any thoughts you have that fall into this category of taboo or unacceptable. (Don't worry—we promise we're not looking.) Or, if you don't feel comfortable writing them in print, type them on a device and then delete them or write them on a separate sheet of paper and tear it up when you're done. Just a little nudge of encouragement here: writing down your thoughts is a great first step in viewing those thoughts more mindfully and observing them as what they really are: simply words in your head (like "hurting my loved one").

_____

_____

_____

_____

_____

What emotions arose as you wrote/typed out those taboo or unacceptable thoughts?

_____

_____

_____

_____

Catastrophic Thoughts

Catastrophic thoughts are negative thoughts about the future, typically involving themes of future disaster, failure, or pain. They also tend to involve the imagined lack of ability to cope. You've probably had the experience of drifting off to sleep and then suddenly becoming aware of the potential for some awful future event such that your entire body jolts awake. These types of thoughts are especially common in GAD and may come in the form of worries about losing one's job or home. Those with health obsessions may be burdened by relentless thoughts of getting a terminal illness. Those with specific phobias may experience thoughts of their fears coming true and being overwhelmed, socially ostracized, or permanently harmed in the process. If you struggle with BPD, you may have thoughts about being hated, rejected, or punished somehow.

When we are immersed in catastrophic thinking, we all make an interesting error: we imagine our present-moment self (the one having the catastrophic thoughts) in the place of our future self (the one who actually has to deal with the catastrophe if it occurs). In reality, we are always changing, learning, and evolving, so it is unknowable how we would cope with a future event. It is this uncertainty that can taunt and torture a susceptible person (imagine how nice it would be to just assume you could cope with whatever arises somehow).

We experience thoughts in the present moment, but catastrophic thoughts are stories about the future that can make it feel like the future is happening now. Imagine coming home to find that your house is engulfed in flames. You might immediately start to think of how hard it is going to be to recover from the personal and financial loss and feel a complex series of intense emotions. Now imagine being at work and simply having a thought about your house catching on fire. Because it can be so easy to get carried away by thoughts, you might experience something very similar, a sudden tensing of the body and a sense that you need to somehow prepare for something dreadful as if it's really happening. Catastrophic thoughts can generate a lot of anxiety and strong urges to worry, seek reassurance, and avoid. They can also put you in a terrible mood because you start to feel what your future self might feel if the catastrophe were to come true.

Take a moment to write down some catastrophic thoughts you experience (for example, *My plane will crash*):

_____

_____

_____

_____

_____

_____

When these thoughts come to mind, how do they make you feel?

_____

_____

_____

_____

Self-Blaming and Self-Critical Thoughts

Intrusive thoughts that come in the form of *I am bad* or *I should have known better* or *It's all my fault!* can be ego-syntonic or ego-dystonic. Negative self-thoughts are extraordinarily common in all the conditions we've discussed. We find ourselves in a bind because we want to have pleasant thoughts and feelings, but we actually have all manner of thoughts and feelings, and so our inability to control this sometimes makes us think we have failed. This may not be easy to read if you are used to blaming yourself for everything and criticizing yourself a lot, but self-blaming and self-critical thoughts all spring from confusion over what we can and cannot control. It may seem perfectly reasonable to beat yourself up when you make a mistake or hurt someone's feelings, but this is really just a product of conditioning and not based on objectively recognizing how we end up doing things we regret.

Put simply, all of our choices, including those that don't work out or don't appear to be in line with our values, are based on what thoughts and feelings preceded the choices. This is an easy test to run—consider the name of *any* song and write it down here:

_____

Good choice! Not as good as "Rocket Man" by Elton John, but respectable. Whatever song you just chose, you have the experience of having chosen it, right? Now carefully consider this next question: Why did you not pick a *different* song? Take a moment to reflect and then write down your answer here:

_____

You may have what seems like a reasonable answer for that question, but the reality is that the *other* song did not show up when you looked for a song. In other words, the thought chose *you* more than you chose the thought. We joked about "Rocket Man" above because that's the song that popped into Jon's head when writing this bit. It could have been "Tiny Dancer," but it wasn't. When we criticize and punish ourselves, we are saying we *should have chosen our experiences differently*, but in fact, this is impossible. We would have had to have been able to choose our thoughts and feelings, and we simply cannot do that. Choice comes in the form of the nature of attention we use right now in *this* moment, not five minutes ago or five minutes from now. By developing skills that help us pay better attention to the present moment, we give ourselves a better shot at making wise-minded choices.

There are many reasons a person may be susceptible to self-blaming and self-critical thinking. Someone with OCD may experience an unwanted intrusive thought that something bad was their fault when it wasn't (like thinking a traffic accident seen on the news was somehow their fault). Someone with BDD may feel so displeased by what they see in the mirror, it feels natural to make negative comments about their appearance. Social interactions that feel uncomfortable may be met with self-critical thoughts about not saying the right thing or assumptions about what other people are thinking. Conditions like BPD and PTSD can drive some people to rely on self-criticism to feel safe.

We imagine that self-blame and self-criticism will produce better behavior and better outcomes, though there is no reason to think this is true. The evidence does not support the idea that punishment is a particularly effective reinforcer. Rather, it teaches us to be sneaky, to avoid punishment, not to make wiser choices. Self-blaming and self-critical thoughts can stir up feelings of guilt, shame, disgust, anxiety, and anger. They can twist us into knots, make us feel like we have to avoid the people and things we love. Above all, self-criticism creates a feedback loop: you have a mean thought about yourself, you feel bad, you have a mean thought about yourself, and so on. In contrast, self-compassion asks the essential question: What would be helpful in this moment? But learning how to respond to these types of thoughts with self-compassion takes effort and skill. We'll do our best to give you some pointers as you move along through this book.

What does it sound like in your head when you are having self-critical thoughts? Perhaps something like: *I am a loser and I always make people uncomfortable.* Write down some examples in your own voice:

_____

_____

_____

What feelings arise when you are being self-critical?

_____

_____

Judgmental Thoughts

We just discussed unkind thoughts toward oneself, but critical and blaming thoughts that are focused outward can also be very upsetting. These thoughts reflect difficulty accepting when things are one way but you really want them to be another, and you imagine other people or institutions (or the universe!) are at fault. They may be. Having anger and judgment toward your least-favorite politicians or the romantic partner who broke your heart is totally normal. Most judgmental thoughts are subject to change when new information comes along. For example, you may judge how slow someone is driving until you see them pull over with a flat tire. Anger, too, often dissipates when an injustice has been resolved or feels less significant over time. Sometimes people have difficulty letting go of judgmental and angry thoughts, so these thoughts continue to intrude and burden them indefinitely to the point of impairment.

Someone with OCD who has been carefully trying not to get contaminated may find themselves having angry thoughts about someone who accidentally contaminated their space. Someone with unwanted taboo obsessions might have angry thoughts about a friend who showed them a movie with triggering scenes in it. A person with panic disorder with agoraphobia may have angry thoughts about a loved one who insisted they come to a concert with them. Someone who finally found a peaceful, pleasant, or safe mental place may become furious at whomever they think triggered them out of it by saying the wrong thing.

Judgmental thoughts often bring up a lot of anger and anxiety. It can feel like a matter of urgency to get the target of your judgment to stop doing what's upsetting you. It can also bring up a lot of shame and self-disgust. *Why am I so judgmental?* You might be minding your own business and then—bam!—a thought about how stupid or selfish or incompetent someone is just hits you like a ton of bricks. How dare they exist and make these thoughts exist too! Many of us have trouble cooling down when anger toward others has us revved up, and until we cool down, we often end up thinking and doing things that make matters worse. This can, of course, result in all of the types of thoughts we discussed above (unacceptable, catastrophic, self-critical) bursting onto the scene as well.

What are some judgmental thoughts that tend to burden you (for example, *I hate my therapist for self-ishly not making more time for me*):

_____

_____

_____

How do these thoughts tend to make you feel?

_____

_____

Checking In

In this chapter, we examined the nature of thoughts and how different types of thoughts impact people with a variety of mental health conditions. We identified an important distinction between ego-dystonic thoughts, which are unwanted, intrusive, and confusing to the thinker, and ego-syntonic thoughts, which can also be unwanted and intrusive, but appear to make sense to the thinker at the time. Lastly, we looked at the types of thoughts people tend to find relentless, unyielding, and especially challenging to navigate and the types of emotions they often conjure up. These include unacceptable or taboo thoughts, catastrophic thoughts, self-critical thoughts, and judgmental thoughts toward others.

In the next chapter, we will explore the world of emotions and the different ways in which people make sense of them.

CHAPTER 2

Understanding Difficult Emotions

Difficulties with emotions and emotion regulation are associated with several psychiatric illnesses, including anxiety disorders, personality disorders, bipolar disorder, major depression, seasonal affective disorder, intermittent explosive disorder, substance abuse, and many others. Furthermore, behavioral disorders and conditions, such as attention-deficit/hyperactivity disorder, can also have emotional symptoms. In this chapter, we pay close attention to and describe the condition of borderline personality disorder because, more than any other psychiatric condition, it presents with and causes the greatest difficulty in emotional experiencing and emotional control.

Something to consider throughout this chapter is that we all have varying degrees of traits of pretty much everything. Picture a sound mixer with all the different levels of all the different sound qualities. We all have an internal equalizer, like an audio engineer's soundboard. You may have one trait that is very high while another is very low. We are using BPD as our main example for a cluster of traits that are very high around emotion dysregulation. You absolutely do not have to have this condition to easily relate to many of its symptoms.

What Are Emotions?

It is one thing to say that you feel "emotional" and another thing to be clear on the actual emotion you're feeling, how it impacts you, and what to do about it. Often when people come to therapy for help dealing with strong emotions, we want them to know what their emotions are and how they are impacting them. When asked, they usually say something like, "I don't know, I'm feeling overwhelmed" or "really upset" or "so angry." They know they don't like how they're feeling in these states, but we want them to be more precise, because it is in the precision that the effectiveness of the solution to strong emotions resides. So as therapists, we persist in wanting to know: "I get that you are overwhelmed, but what specific emotions are you feeling right now?"

One of the most frequent responses we get to that question is: "Wait, what? How would I know? How would I figure that out?"

We ask them to pay attention to their experience, but even this seems daunting and abstract, especially when we're asking them to closely attend to something experienced as painful and aversive. If you've ever been to therapy, did you go thinking, *I hope this makes these feelings go away?* Before you are able to pay attention to what you feel, however, you first need to know what you are looking for and how to describe it.

Primary Emotions

Before we look further into emotions, let's define the term "cue." One way of thinking about a cue is that it is a stimulus, an event, or an object that is significant to us and that subsequently causes a change in our behavior or experience. One of the things that a cue can cause is an emotion. For instance, if a snarling dog comes up and bares its teeth (the cue), that can cause the emotion of fear to arise. In this particular case, fear would be a primary emotion. Cues can be internal or external. In the situation of the dog, that is an external cue. An example of an internal cue would be a thought you have about yourself.

Primary emotions are the ones that show up immediately after encountering the cue—the emotions you feel first. Emotions are produced by nerves and chemicals in the brain in response to a cue. Primary emotions are hardwired into the brains of nearly all human beings, regardless of race or culture, and are associated with facial and behavioral expressions. The theory is that we evolved to have these primary emotions as survival mechanisms. For instance, the face of disgust is universal and signals to the self and others that something—say, a food—may be rotten. The face of fear signals to the self and others that something dangerous is in the environment.

We have ten primary emotions:

1. **Joy:** a feeling of happiness or contentment

2. **Love:** an intense feeling of deep affection

3. **Sadness:** a feeling of sorrow, grief, or unhappiness

4. **Anger:** a strong feeling of annoyance, irritation, or hostility

5. **Fear:** a strong feeling that something or someone is dangerous and will cause harm

6. **Guilt:** a feeling of having done something wrong in a way that has opposed a personal value

7. **Shame:** a feeling of painful humiliation or distress caused by behavior that has opposed societal norms or values

8. **Envy:** an unsettling feeling of discontentment caused by the desire to have or possess something that somebody else has, whether a tangible object or a personal attribute

9. **Jealousy:** a feeling of uneasiness that can arise from suspicion or fear of rivalry; in particular, that the rival will take from us something that is deeply important to us

10. **Disgust:** a feeling of revulsion

Take a moment to reflect on these emotions and how they show up for you. Which emotions do you find particularly intense or challenging?

Secondary Emotions

In the mental health field, secondary emotions are defined as the emotional reactions we have to other emotions. For example, if a person is rejected, they may feel angry as a result of initially having felt sad. In this case, sadness would be the primary emotion and anger would be the secondary emotion.

Secondary emotions are often caused by the beliefs we have about experiencing the primary emotion. A person may think that sadness is a reflection of being weak and then lash out in anger. And so, whenever these emotions are experienced, thoughts come up and, in turn, trigger secondary emotions.

Do you ever notice secondary emotions coming along with the primary emotions you just identified above? Take note of that experience here:

What Causes Emotional Problems?

At the start of this chapter, we listed several mental health conditions that involve difficulty with emotions. It stands to reason that if you don't have difficulty in controlling your emotions, you likely won't be someone seeking help for emotional symptoms from a mental health professional. On the other hand, many people with mental health problems often present to their primary care clinician as a first point of contact if they have worries about their overall mental health, and sometimes emotional problems are a manifestation of medical conditions.

In other words, emotional problems are not always simply a reflection of mental health conditions. Medications and substances can directly impact many parts of the nervous system, including the emotional centers in the brain. Medical conditions, such as traumatic brain injury, can contribute to emotional symptoms by damaging brain tissue.

Of course, even for people who do not have mental health diagnoses, there are situations and environmental factors that can lead to significant difficulties in controlling emotions, such as physical, emotional, or sexual trauma, the loss of a loved one, loss of a job, or a divorce. In many cases, as time goes on, the emotional symptoms typically, but not always, resolve.

What Is Borderline Personality Disorder?

The most common mental health condition that causes people to have the experience of rapidly changing and roller-coaster-like symptoms is borderline personality disorder. You may not have BPD, but you may have some of the emotional problems associated with BPD, and so you may benefit from the skills we'll be relaying in this book to manage these emotions. The skills are so effective that they can work for almost anyone willing to try them, whether they have a mental health condition or not.

BPD is a common mental health condition that impacts the way you think and feel about yourself and others. It is characterized by a difficulty in managing emotions that can lead to self-destructive behavior and unstable relationships. The instability in relationships is often triggered by fear of being abandoned or of being alone. But in a kind of cruel irony, the difficulty in controlling emotions and related mood swings can push others away and lead to the very abandonment you fear.

Marsha Linehan, PhD, author of the 1993 seminal book *Cognitive-Behavioral Treatment of Borderline Personality Disorder* and developer of dialectical behavior therapy, a treatment used for people who have difficulties in regulating their emotions, identified five types of dysregulation that affect people with BPD:

1. **Emotion dysregulation** is characterized by difficulty in effectively managing emotions. You may relate to the experience of being thrown around by your emotions and then behaving in ways driven by strong and rapidly changing feelings. This is called *mood-dependent behavior* and is often inconsistent with a person's values or long-term goals, leading to more difficult emotions, such as guilt and shame.

2. **Interpersonal dysregulation** is the experience of chaos in close relationships. Frequently, there is difficulty managing and maintaining relationships, coupled with the fear of being abandoned by the important people in your life. This can be caused by, or lead to, more emotion dysregulation.

3. **Self-dysregulation** is the experience of not seeing oneself as a whole, integrated person and instead struggling to define and clarify a sense of self. It is characterized by an instability in, or rapidly changing, core values, core identity, self-image, long-term goals, and ideologies. It can lead to feelings of loneliness, boredom, and emptiness. Have you ever asked the question "Who even am I?" and felt thrown by the silence that followed?

4. **Behavioral dysregulation** is the inability to effectively control the behaviors that are driven by strong emotions. It is characterized by the use of behaviors like self-injury, suicidality, exposure to dangerous sexual situations, misuse of drugs and alcohol, disordered eating, dangerous driving, and other potentially life-threatening behaviors to control intolerable emotional states.

5. **Cognitive dysregulation** is the experience of problems in thinking and problem solving. It includes engaging in *cognitive distortions*, which are exaggerated patterns of thought in which conclusions are often not based on fact. Cognitive dysregulation consequently leads people to view things more negatively than they really are and see life in inflexible all-or-nothing terms. (We will explore cognitive distortions more fully in the chapters ahead.)

What Are the Signs and Symptoms of Emotional Control Problems?

Emotional experiences can occur at any time. They can be experienced as positive or negative, wanted or unwanted. Emotional changes can be normal, and typically, they are temporary responses to events or cues. However, when emotions are disproportionate or excessive, extreme in intensity, persistent or unstable, or difficult to control, they can indicate an underlying problem or disorder.

People who have difficulty in regulating their emotions can experience a roller coaster of mood shifts from depression to anxiety to anger. Sometimes these shifts happen in a matter of minutes or hours. Anxiety, shame, and guilt can quickly turn to urges to avoid these feelings with compulsions or use of self-harm or substances as a way to diminish the impact of the emotions. Often, intense and volatile emotions can be experienced as unpredictable and even scary to other people, which can lead to significant relationship problems.

There is another side to controlling excessive emotions. Some people, because of having had negative experiences with high emotions, go to great lengths to suppress their emotions. So rather than having too many emotions, they can come across as having none. Emotional suppression can be very dangerous. It is the equivalent of holding a lid on a boiling pot of water. Eventually, suppressing can become too much.

What Other Symptoms Might Occur with Emotional Symptoms?

Emotional symptoms may accompany other symptoms that vary depending on the underlying disease, disorder, or condition. The nervous system controls the whole body, and so emotional problems are not simply experiences in the head. Conditions that frequently affect the emotions may also involve other body systems, including:

- **Gastrointestinal tract:** leading to appetite and weight changes, nausea and vomiting, and changes in bowel movements

- **Respiratory system:** leading to persistent cough, shortness of breath, and flu-like symptoms

- **Urinary system:** leading to incontinence or needing to urinate frequently

- **Overall body:** leading to insomnia, feeling fatigued and generally ill, with various aches and pains

When you are having difficulty with your emotions, where in your body is impacted?

_____

_____

What If Emotional Control Problems Become Very Serious?

Emotions such as extreme sadness (with aggression) or agitation (with feelings of emptiness), guilt, helplessness, and hopelessness can all lead to a sense of loss of control over one's life. A person who experiences a complete loss of control is more prone to accidents, poor decision making, and, at times, self-harm, the contemplation of suicide, and even violence toward others.

As with any psychological or physical symptom, serious problems can arise. If they become life-threatening, emergency care (such as calling 911 in the United States or going to a hospital emergency room or urgent care clinic) should always be considered. Situations considered emergencies include:

- A threat or action to act on suicidal thoughts

- A threat or action to assault another person

- An inability to care for oneself due to excessive emotional problems impairing judgment

- A very rapid and unexplained change in mental state, such as sudden states of confusion, hallucinations (hearing voices or seeing things that others don't see), or sudden lethargy or sleepiness that may indicate ingestion of dangerous substances

What Questions Should Be Asked to Assess the Impact of Emotional Problems?

As therapists, there are certain questions we are interested in asking as we assess the impact and scope of emotional problems:

- When did you first notice your emotional symptoms?

- Did you notice them, or did someone in your life point them out?

- How would you describe your symptoms?

- Does anything make them better or worse?

- When do they typically occur?

- Do you have any psychiatric or medical problems?

- Do you take medications?

- Do you drink any alcohol or use recreational drugs?

- Have the emotional problems led to significant consequences, such as loss of relationships, a job, inability to finish school, accidents, and so on?

If someone presents with new difficulties in emotions and there's no obvious cause and they've previously been healthy, we will often request that the person get a physical examination with their primary care physician, just to make sure that the emotional symptoms aren't being caused by a medical problem.

Checking In

In this chapter, we looked at the complex and mysterious world of human emotions. You may have had some emotions yourself while reading it (hopefully, not all uncomfortable ones!). We examined the difference between primary and secondary emotions, as well as some of the challenges people face when they have difficulty controlling or containing emotions.

In the next chapter, we switch gears to look at specific strategies for dealing with unwanted thoughts that might elicit strong emotions.

CHAPTER 3

The Fundamentals of CBT and ERP for Unwanted Thoughts

Even before we learn to speak, we naturally know to go toward what pleases us and away from what causes us pain. A child may touch a hot stove out of curiosity, but burnt fingers teach a powerful lesson not to do that twice. What are we to do, though, when the painful object—the hot stove, as it were—exists in our minds?

You've likely had the experience of recognizing a thought that triggers acute mental pain and then finding yourself very motivated to avoid the things that bring on that thought. If those things cannot be avoided, you may find yourself strategizing a variety of ways to suppress or neutralize the thought when it arises. As the thought keeps coming up, you keep recoiling, and over time, your world gets smaller and smaller. Too many things cause you to become aware of the unwanted thought, and too many efforts at avoidance cause you to sacrifice the things you value.

When our efforts to flee our unwanted thoughts begin to cause impairment, we call this condition, well, a "condition." Earlier, we named a few of the most common conditions that involve unwanted thoughts and difficulty with emotions. Evidence-based treatments for these conditions fall under the umbrella of cognitive behavioral therapy.

CBT

Cognitive is a term that refers to thoughts and thinking, so cognitive approaches to psychotherapy look at the way we relate to our thoughts and ask us to consider making changes in perspective that are more likely to lead to healthy behaviors. *Behavioral* approaches look at the individual actions we take and invite us to learn from the experience of choosing different actions. Cognitive behavioral therapy—CBT—combines these two concepts to help us better understand how what we are thinking relates to what we are feeling and what we are doing with those feelings.

Cognitive Tools

The cognitive skills that are used in addressing unwanted thoughts involve recognizing the way we are thinking about our experiences that may be leading us to unhelpful conclusions, thus driving up painful emotions we'd very much rather avoid. As mentioned in chapter 2 when discussing cognitive dysregulation, these unhelpful thinking strategies are known as *cognitive distortions*, meaning they are ways of thinking that have a negative impact on our ability to remain objective. Here are a few of the most common cognitive distortions that tend to make the experience of unwanted thoughts harder to navigate:

- **All-or-nothing thinking:** looking at your experience as being only one way or its opposite instead of viewing it on a spectrum

- **Catastrophizing:** predicting a negative outcome and assuming you won't be able to cope with it

- **Magnifying:** framing your experience in exaggerated terms, making it bigger than it would otherwise be

- **Overgeneralizing:** taking information from one experience and applying it across the board to many or all experiences

- **Discounting the positive:** disregarding or disqualifying evidence that your experience may be tolerable

- **Emotional reasoning:** assuming that the content of your unwanted thoughts is true primarily because of the feelings that come alongside it

- **Selective abstraction:** overfocusing on content that relates to your unwanted thoughts without taking in the bigger picture

- **Should/must statements:** taking an overly rigid or perfectionist stance on your thoughts and feelings

- **Personalizing:** attributing the behavior of others to your own unwanted thoughts and feelings

- **Mind reading:** assuming that others are thinking things about you that are unwanted

- **Thought-action fusion:** believing that having thoughts about an act is the same thing as doing that act

Cognitive therapy (or the C in CBT) can be helpful in challenging some of the initial assumptions that may arise in your mind, allowing you to look more objectively at what's troubling you and make wiser decisions in how to respond.

For each of the cognitive distortions below, see if you can come up with an example of a thought you have that aligns with that process. For example, *My hands are either perfectly clean or unacceptably dirty* is a good representation of all-or-nothing thinking. As you practice, you may notice that some distortions resonate more than others and, of course, you may not engage in some at all.

IDENTIFY COGNITIVE DISTORTIONS	
Cognitive Distortion	Example
All-or-nothing thinking	
Catastrophizing	
Magnifying	
Overgeneralizing	
Discounting the positive	
Emotional reasoning	
Selective abstraction	
Should/must statements	
Personalizing	
Mind reading	
Thought-action fusion	

The problem with cognitive distortions is that they confuse us into thinking we have a project to solve that we actually cannot solve, usually the changing of the past, the predicting of the future, or the obtaining of certainty about something. Let's call this the "false project." Instead, it would be more effective to focus on the problems that we *can* solve—namely, addressing the present moment, coping with our hard feelings, and accepting uncertainty. We'll call this the "real project."

There's a tool people can use to help them recognize and challenge cognitive distortions: the automatic thought record. We've created a modified thought record here for you to practice recognizing how your thoughts make you feel and how both your thoughts and feelings can sometimes keep you from addressing your needs in the present moment. Following the model of the examples given, try this out for yourself with some of the thoughts and feelings you've been grappling with recently.

ERP

In the world of OCD and related disorders, the core behavioral treatment is exposure and response prevention. ERP involves intentionally interacting with the things that bring on your unwanted thoughts (exposure) while resisting efforts to neutralize those thoughts (response prevention). If you understand the problem behind your struggle with intrusive thoughts, then it is easy to understand the solution. Efforts to stop unwanted thoughts teach the brain that these thoughts are especially threatening. Efforts to allow these thoughts to arise and pass by teach the brain that these thoughts are less significant.

A useful way to think about this is to remember that the brain itself, an organ in your body, has no opinion on the intrinsic meaning of your thoughts. Remarkably, in the moment Jon was writing this section, he had an experience that captured this concept. A client had asked Jon to talk to someone on her behalf because she was afraid she would be misunderstood. Jon agreed but cautioned that, ultimately, she would have to be the one to get her needs heard in that relationship. As he sat down to work on this section of the book, he got a new email alert and habitually opened it. Here is what it said:

Jon, I think it was a cop-out for you to—

At this point, Jon's chest began to tighten, a lump appeared in his throat, heat radiated from his chin to his scalp. He'd let someone down! They were disappointed! He'd made someone's life worse by failing to do something or …

—have to be the one to talk to her on my behalf. I'm going to do this myself and take responsibility for what happens next. Thank you for your encouragement.

FALSE PROJECT vs. REAL PROJECT
MODIFIED AUTOMATIC THOUGHT RECORD

Triggering Thought	Accompanying Feelings	Cognitive Distortion(s)	False Project (the impossible-to-solve problem)	Real Project (the present-moment issue to address)
I'm going to get sick	Anxiety	Catastrophizing	Prove I won't get sick in the future	Cope with not knowing if I'll get sick
My friend hates me because they didn't return my text	Self-loathing	Mind reading, personalizing, all-or-nothing thinking	Get my friend to return my text—show them how much pain they caused me	Find compassion for myself while I sit with this; remember I don't know why my friend hasn't replied

Suddenly, the heat drained from Jon's face, the lump disappeared from his throat, and the weight pressing down on his chest simply vanished. Between the beginning and the end of a single sentence, conditioned thoughts and feelings had taken Jon on a wild ride.

Has this ever happened to you? No? Just Jon? Okay, but still, it illustrates an important point: emotions can be so closely associated with thoughts that before we even take the time to recognize what we are thinking, we may already start to feel the interpretation of a thought. Do thoughts cause emotions, or do emotions become attached to thoughts and then we start to relate to those thoughts like they have power to change how we feel?

Consider your reaction to the following words: "tree," "desk," "seeing," "sweater."

Now consider your reaction to these words: "cancer," "stabbing," "pedophile," "poison."

Most likely, you had a neutral reaction to the first list and a negative (slight or significant) reaction to the second. Yet the lists are actually identical in that they are merely ink on paper (or dots on a screen if you're reading this digitally or sounds on a speaker if you're listening to the audiobook!) followed by stories you have learned about these concepts.

Let's try an experiment. Take out a piece of paper and write any neutral word on it—any word at all. Stare at the word for a bit, then ask yourself, *What am I looking at?* If you wrote the word "cat," for example, what do you see? Is it an actual cat? Of course not. Is it a word? Well, it is to you if you speak the language and understand the symbols. Are the letters symbols? How do you know that? In the end, what you are looking at is nothing but ink on paper. Now do this again, but this time with a word you identify as an unwanted thought. What are you really looking at?

The brain learns how to relate to thoughts largely by our behavior. It doesn't always know to bring on anxiety in response to any given scary thought until your behavior around the thought shows the brain that the thought is related to something dangerous. Or put more simply, if you avoid something, your brain learns that this thing needs to be avoided because it might harm you otherwise. When you try to reengage with that same thing, you will receive a reminder from the brain: *Alert: possible danger.* Your brain is designed to assume you know what you're doing, not that you are guided by distorted thinking, so you must be avoiding your trigger for a good reason.

Taken a step further, imagine something causes you distress and then you find something that immediately and reliably takes that distress away. The next time you experience distress in response to that thing, your brain will remind you to engage in the same behavior that took your distress away. This concept is called *negative reinforcement*, and it is the driving force behind most conditions that involve unwanted thoughts and feelings. "Negative" because it removes something, and "reinforcement" because it causes something to be more likely to be repeated. It follows, then, that when you try to do anything other than the behavior that relieves your distress, you become, well, even more distressed than before! Your brain has learned how to keep you safe and is going to react to anything that violates that.

Take a moment to track this with your own thoughts and feelings. Write down a thought you find particularly intrusive or difficult to experience:

_____

When you notice the thought, what emotion tends to come along with it? _____

What behavior do you engage in to try to make yourself feel better, safer, or more certain?

_____

What happens with the thoughts and feelings when you don't engage in that behavior?

_____

If the feelings get worse, what leads you to the conclusion that you must escape them? You can include thoughts about it being too hard, symptoms of panic, or any other observable experience that comes up in this space:

_____

_____

_____

_____

Changing the way you respond to unwanted thoughts and feelings is hard because your brain essentially resists letting go of what has been reinforced. You may have written above that you experience more anxiety or disgust or some other unpleasant experience in reaction to an unwanted thought. Naturally, you feel pressure to get away from those feelings, but avoidance and other rituals keep reinforcing that the feelings are intolerable and that the thoughts must be important. Therefore, treatment for conditions that involve unwanted thoughts and feelings often focuses on *eliminating* that reinforcement. Rather than repeatedly learning that we must respond compulsively to unwanted thoughts, we can learn that unwanted thoughts are not fundamentally threatening or intolerable. They are thoughts. Put simply, ERP exposes us to the conditions that make us want to do compulsions and then we show the brain that we can be in that space *without* engaging in those compulsions.

Think of your email account: a ton of unwanted messages (spam) are filtered into your junk mail folder. Yet some of those messages occasionally end up in your regular inbox. A computer algorithm helps to determine what goes into junk mail and what goes into the inbox. It learns this, in part, from how you relate to the emails. If you tag them as spam without reading them or ignore them altogether, they are more likely to be labeled as spam. If you open them, read them, and even *reply* to them (yikes!), you teach the algorithm to send more messages like that directly to your inbox. ERP is a strategy for improving the algorithm as it relates to your mental spam.

Habituation and Inhibitory Learning

Two types of learning can take place when we engage in exposure and response prevention with our unwanted thoughts: *habituation* and *inhibitory learning*. Habituation simply means a decrease in a behavioral response when repeatedly presented with the same stimuli. If you have unwanted thoughts about getting contaminated from touching a pen and you repeatedly touch a pen without washing your hands, eventually you will feel less and less "dirty" when touching the pen. This makes sense because the feeling of being "dirty" is only present in the first place to compel you to wash. In the absence of washing (or anything else that would eliminate the feeling), there is no reason for the brain to persist with the message of "dirty."

That said, not everyone who engages in ERP experiences much habituation despite their best efforts, and this may have something to do with the way in which people learn to fear things. When a fear first develops, there is a connection between the fear trigger and the unbearable urge to escape it. In other words, when you encounter what triggers you, the brain points you straight to the "make it stop!" position and you *expect* not to be able to handle it. However, when you use ERP to intentionally encounter your fear trigger while *violating* that expectation, new learning takes place. This new, or "inhibitory," learning means you have paired the fear trigger with less-threatening associations. Over time, you feel less compelled to respond to your thoughts with compulsions because you have demonstrated multiple times that your expectation of failure (or of the inability to cope) is inaccurate, even if it is still distressing. If you touch multiple pens in multiple places at multiple difficulty levels, you learn to be inhibited from responding to them only like they are contaminated. You may or may not feel dirty, but you don't feel compelled to put an end to it.

Myths About ERP

A powerful myth about ERP is that it is dangerous, especially for people with difficulty regulating emotions, such as those who struggle with BPD. The thinking goes that with exposure to unwanted thoughts, which is likely to bring on challenging emotions, someone predisposed to being dysregulated by these experiences is going to act out inappropriately, harm themselves, or be retraumatized. This myth, like many, is problematic because it presumes an inability on the part of the person with intense emotions to utilize any skills that might be helpful. The central thesis of this book is that exposure-based interventions can be done safely and wisely for people with intense emotions as long as they're given the appropriate skills for staying in the productive part of the challenging experience.

Exposure-based treatments take courage and attitude, no doubt about that. But you may have an association with the word "exposure" that is synonymous with torture, another myth. Exposure therapy gets a reputation for cruelty because of the way it may be portrayed in the media or implemented by well-intentioned but misguided therapists. It is true that, in some cases, overcorrection, or doing something more than "normal," can be helpful in generating the new learning necessary in overcoming unwanted thoughts. For example, a person with BDD who fears a part of their body is unattractive may practice exposure to that by wearing an article of clothing that highlights that part of the body. They might not normally do that, but going out of the way to do more than just resisting avoidance can be a powerful way to change how the brain responds to the thoughts involved. But it is important to remember that these overcorrection strategies should never be cruel, forced, or self-punitive. They are, instead, invitations to rediscover your resolve, courage, and strength.

Another troubling myth about exposure is that it is superficial, that it fails to get at the root of one's suffering. This myth comes from a misconception that top-down approaches (treating behaviors) are less meaningful than bottom-up approaches (treating underlying beliefs and contexts first). There is very little reason to take this myth seriously. Because exposure asks us to enter new territory, to choose actions that defy our instincts, it calls for digging deeper into the center of our souls and then, rather than stop there, taking a step forward into a better life.

While exposure is a step toward what scares you, response prevention is how your brain learns you are more competent and capable than you once believed. Without response prevention, exposure does very little. Touching something dirty with gloves on won't teach you that you can handle uncertainty any more than watching a scary movie with the sound off and your eyes closed will teach you that you can handle disturbing thoughts. But resisting compulsions is not about "white-knuckling" through an experience. Hold your breath, grin and bear it, don't look down, just do it quickly, remember it'll be over soon—this all sounds like good advice, but these messages teach the brain that what you're doing cannot be tolerated as is. The whole purpose behind your efforts needs to be to establish a pattern of "I can do this" and not "This is bigger than me."

Finally, a particularly unhelpful myth around response prevention is that *any* effort to reduce distress in the face of unwanted thoughts and feelings is inherently compulsive. This is untrue for a few reasons. A compulsion is an attempt to be certain about the content of your unwanted thoughts (including the unwanted thought that your feelings will annihilate you). While any behavior *could* function as a compulsion, using coping and regulating skills is not inherently compulsive. Taking a deep breath, engaging in a valued behavior, meditating, exercising, and practicing mindfulness more generally can all be strategies for staying in the mental and emotional state where the most learning can take place.

Drawing on specific therapy tools that complement ERP can be essential for making it work. If an exposure is not activating at all, the brain does not pick up on the experience as new learning. However, if an exposure is so dysregulating that you enter a state of panic or dissociation, the brain is also not in a state of taking on new learning. Learning to regulate within the context of an exposure is the key to staying in the zone long enough to learn how to overcome your challenges (which is where DBT skills come into the mix, as you'll see in the next chapter).

How to Make ERP Work

If we expect to see changes in our relationship to things that scare us, we can't expect to do this simply by talking about them. Earlier, we explored the intended aims of ERP: the reduction of distress (habituation) and the reduction of the need to flee distress (inhibitory learning). There's your "what" and your "why;" now we'll discuss the "how."

But before we dig into the core strategies used in ERP, a few important guidelines:

- Exposures are never intentionally dangerous and should never involve putting yourself in situations where actual harm is likely to occur.

- Exposures never need to go against your religion or values.

- Exposures are effective only when paired with meaningful response prevention (resisting physical and mental compulsions).

- Exposures are effective only when you are a present witness to them (not in a state of panic, dissociation, or intoxication).

Types of Exposure Techniques

Exposure, or intentionally encountering the things that scare you, can be done in a variety of ways.

In Vivo ERP

Directly encountering the fear trigger is called *in vivo* ERP: going up against what scares you in real life. If you have a fear of contamination, you might build an in vivo hierarchy that looks something like this:

1. Be in the room several feet from the contaminant without doing compulsions.

2. Stand near the contaminant.

3. Touch an object that has been near the contaminant.

4. Touch the contaminant using a barrier (e.g., a tissue).

5. Touch a contaminated barrier from a previous exposure.

6. Touch the contaminant directly with one finger.

7. Touch the contaminant directly with your whole hand.

8. Touch the contaminant directly to other parts of your clothes or body.

9. Cross-contaminate objects to other areas of your personal possessions or home.

10. Engage in "clean" activities with contaminated hands.

In vivo ERP doesn't only mean touching things, of course. It often means putting yourself in situations that will reliably trigger your unwanted thoughts. A person with a fear of germs may do in vivo ERP being in a public restroom, whether they touch anything or not. Along these lines, a person afraid of causing harm can do in vivo ERP by going to a place where it would be possible to cause harm (like a subway platform) while resisting compulsions. Here are some in vivo ideas that could be helpful for different fears:

Contamination

- Touching contaminated items

- Being in places where the presence of the contaminant is guaranteed or likely

- Wearing contaminated clothes

- Using contaminated objects for their intended purpose

Harm-Related Obsessions

- Using triggering objects (e.g., a knife) for their intended purpose

- Being in environments where causing harm would be easy

- Watching triggering media that reliably brings on thoughts of harm

Unacceptable Thoughts/Taboo Obsessions

- Being around triggering people or objects

- Watching triggering media that brings on unwanted thoughts

- Engaging in otherwise valued activities despite them bringing on unwanted thoughts

Symmetry/Just-Right/Perfectionism Obsessions

- Doing things intentionally imperfectly or "wrong"

- Engaging in tasks of precision or competition without trying to master them

Social and Appearance-Based Fears

- Being in social environments that may be triggering

- Volunteering to speak in class, a group, or in public

- Wearing clothes or hairstyles that may bring on thoughts of judgment from others

- Participating in activities that may bring on thoughts of judgment

Relationship Obsessions

- Doing romantic things that may bring on thoughts of doubt in the relationship

- Putting up pictures or social media posts that trigger reminders of the relationship fears

These are but a few examples for a small range of intrusive thoughts, but the key takeaway here is that, in most cases, there are ways to apply strategic exposures in real life to what scares us.

Imaginal ERP

For many unwanted thoughts, there are real and concrete ways to bring them up for in vivo ERP, but for some types of thoughts, finding real-life opportunities can be difficult. In addition, some real-life exposures fail to generate the emotional intensity of the scary stories in our head. So another way to practice exposure is to use writing to generate a story of the unwanted thoughts and feelings.

Imaginal ERP, sometimes called "scripting," typically includes writing about your fear as if it might come true or as if you might experience it coming true. In prolonged exposure for PTSD and for intrusive thoughts that involve real past events, the script might simply be an objective account of what happened so you can practice being with that event in mind and without doing compulsions. For scripts about future or theoretical concerns, you might write a description of the unwanted event occurring and how its unwanted consequences might affect you.

There is no perfect way to compose imaginal exposure scripts. Different tones and styles may be more or less triggering for you. For example, writing about an obsession coming true in the affirmative (e.g., *I will go to the party and they will laugh at me*) may be more or less triggering than writing about it as if it is happening (*I am at the party and people are laughing at me*) or as if it might happen (*I may go to the party and people may laugh at me*). What's most important in using this technique, just like with in vivo ERP, is that it not involve compulsions.

Compulsions to resist during imaginal ERP:

- Writing in reassurance statements that the fear is really untrue

- Writing in rationalizations for why the thought probably won't come true

- Ruminating in your head about whether the script is true while writing or reading it

A script can be any length and is typically something you would read repeatedly as your distress over it goes down. Another strategy would be to write a fresh script every time rather than repeatedly read the same one. The way you want to conceptualize this is that the script is the story of your unwanted thoughts and the goal of exposure to the script is to demonstrate to the brain that it is, in fact, a story—something you can read without doing compulsions or being harmed. Then, when the unwanted thoughts intrude and you start to ruminate over them, your brain remembers: *Wait, this is that story, and we don't need to focus on that right now.*

Scripts can also be used to build motivation for ERP. A lighter, less intense way to use imaginal exposure is to simply write a description of an obsession you are going to stop trying to get certainty about and a reflection on the things you value that make it worthwhile to do this hard work. But again, if these things are going to be effective, it is essential that you not write in any reassurance statements because those will send the signal to your brain that your intrusive thoughts are indeed threatening.

Interoceptive ERP

Another form of exposure focuses on intentionally generating the body state you experience when triggered by your unwanted thoughts. If DBT and related skills can be used to down-regulate internal experiences, interoceptive exposures can be used to up-regulate them for exposure. In many ways, interoceptive exposures are like the opposite of DBT skills, so it's important to approach them gently if you are predisposed to overwhelm.

Interoceptive ERP is most commonly used in exposure to panic symptoms for people who are afraid of having a panic attack and have a tendency toward overresponding to physical sensations they associate with panic. Some examples include breathing through a small straw (providing the illusion of shortness of breath), spinning in a chair and suddenly stopping (to generate dizziness), or running in place (to generate increased heart rate). As always, when these symptoms are pulled up, the goal is to let them come down *without* doing physical or mental rituals and let the brain be a witness to the age-old rule: what goes up must come down. Of course, with any exposure that involves the body, consult with a medical professional to ensure that none of your exposures are risking actual physical harm or exacerbation of a medical condition.

Here are some other ways interoceptive ERP may be useful for addressing unwanted thoughts and feelings:

- Wearing warm clothing on a hot day to generate unwanted sensations of flushness or sweatiness

- Placing a weight on the chest to simulate feelings of dread

- Being in the dark or in an enclosed place for related fears

- Safely drinking an amount of caffeine that can create a jittery or impulsive feeling for related fears

As always, ERP is going to be most effective within a sweet spot of difficulty, where you are distressed enough to make contact with what you fear in your head but not so distressed that you put yourself in danger or otherwise cannot pay attention to the exposure.

Eliminating Compulsions

It cannot be stressed enough that the main component in changing your relationship to unwanted thoughts is, well, *changing* your relationship to unwanted thoughts! When we respond to what scares us with certainty-seeking compulsions, we teach (and reteach) the brain that these thoughts and feelings are fundamentally dangerous. Just as anything can be an obsession, pretty much anything can be a compulsion if its goal is to make you feel more certain. Here are just five categories of compulsions to watch out for (or responses to prevent, the literal meaning of ERP).

Avoidance

Perhaps the most common compulsion, and understandably so, is simply not doing what you care about because of your unwanted thoughts. While avoiding triggers may be an important aspect of staying safe in some contexts (like avoiding things that trigger an urge to use substances when in addiction recovery), avoiding valued behaviors that include your triggers only teaches the brain that your triggers are more powerful than you are.

Avoidance is a first line defense for anything threatening, but it's important to remember that the brain has difficulty telling what's really dangerous from what's simply scary. It learns a lot from the effort you put into avoidance. Here are some ways you may be avoiding experiences:

- Staying away from environments where unwanted thoughts could arise

- Changing the channel when something triggering comes on TV or the radio

- Evading thoughts and feelings through excessive distraction or zoning out (such as mindless video games)

- Shirking responsibilities that may include triggers (not cleaning up because of a fear of contaminants)

- Avoiding words or numbers that might trigger unwanted thoughts and feelings

Avoidance is likely going to be the first compulsion addressed in ERP since any reduction in avoidance is essentially exposure itself.

Reassurance

The unknown can be scary, and humans in general are pretty adept at "knowing skills," meaning we are good at collecting information and using it to make sense of our experiences. The invention of the internet created an environment in which we can collect information (of a wide variety of legitimacy) anytime we want about nearly everything. Although a one-time reality check can be a useful assurance (for example, you can't get HIV from someone's sweat), multiple attempts to repeat this assurance send the signal to your brain that you are not sure and not capable of tolerating uncertainty.

Resisting reassurance can be very difficult. Unfortunately, seeking reassurance robs you of the opportunity to overcome your fears. Here are some ways to compulsively seek reassurance:

- Asking someone to tell you (again) why your fear is untrue

- Googling or otherwise researching evidence that your fear is untrue

- Mentally repeating reassuring information (repeatedly reminding yourself that your COVID test was negative)

- Bringing up the same topic repeatedly to get someone to volunteer reassuring information (like asking your partner how they feel about you so you can hear them say "I love you")

Resisting online searches may necessitate some strategic avoidance, such as limiting the time you allow yourself on a computer or smartphone. And if someone else is on the receiving end of your reassurance seeking, you can enlist their help by forming a contract that helps the other person know how to respond to you and gives them permission to deny you reassurance.

Accommodation

Exposure therapy is going to be less effective when the people around you facilitate your compulsive behavior. Accommodation of the symptoms of OCD and related disorders happens in many families and can show up in several ways, including but not limited to:

- Providing reassurance

- Waiting for you to finish your rituals

- Providing materials for compulsions (like doing extra laundry or buying extra soap for someone with contamination obsessions)

- Facilitating avoidance (like hiding kitchen knives from someone with harm-based fears)

- Endlessly enduring deep analysis discussions about your fears

Neutralizing Behaviors

Many types of compulsive behaviors are attempts to remove or replace triggering thoughts and feelings. There are too many possible compulsions to list, but examples that aim to neutralize triggers include:

- Checking compulsions

- Washing compulsions

- Replacing "bad" thoughts with "good" ones

- "Fixing" things that appear triggering (such as making something symmetrical or adjusting something to a "good" number)

Rumination

Perhaps the most insidious of compulsions, rumination involves intentionally trying to figure out (or get certainty about) your unwanted thoughts. You may be accustomed to hearing and saying things like "I'm obsessing all day," but what we tend to call "obsessing" is actually better understood as *compulsing*. Consider the last time you were triggered by a relentlessly intrusive thought. Immediately thereafter, you very likely took your attention away from what you were doing before the trigger and put your attention on the trigger and its meaning. You very likely then spent some amount of time trying to figure out what the trigger meant and whether or not it was going to harm you.

When you engage in ERP, you may feel strong urges to think about what you're doing and analyze whether or not it's going to work out for you. This is a natural instinct, of course, as is washing your hands when you feel dirty; but when you're trying to create new learning in the brain, rumination gets in the way. Here are some ways rumination can occur:

- Bringing up a thought in your mind for the purpose of analyzing how you feel about it

- Mentally replaying memories, conversations, instructions, dreams, or other mental events until they feel resolved

- Mentally rehearsing upcoming events (excessively repeating to yourself what you are going to say when you see someone)

- Playing out hypothetical scenarios in your head (imagining what would happen if your fears came true *not* when writing an exposure script)

- Mentally debating the significance or meaning of your unwanted thoughts

Baby Steps and Hierarchies

It is important to approach ERP wisely. Much like building muscle mass at the gym, starting with too heavy a weight is likely to cause injury. Starting with too intense an exposure is simply going to result in overwhelm. In a state of total dysregulation, without Olympic coping skills, you are unlikely to learn that you are capable of handling what scares you. Starting with a "weight" that is challenging but manageable is important in the mind just as it is in the gym. Let yourself get the form right, show yourself how strong you are now, then build on that. The key is to establish a new habit of nonavoidance, building exposure muscles to a point where you can be present with what challenges you and very little in life can take you down.

A good way to sort out where to begin is to keep a record of your triggers, how distressing they are, and how you are responding to them. Consider the target fear you want to address with ERP and use the table below to write down some of the triggers you remember encountering over the last few days (column 1), how much they bothered you on a scale of 1 to 10 (column 2), and what behaviors you engaged in to get away from that distress (column 3). Be sure to include in the third column not only the physical behaviors, but also the mental behaviors (ways you tried to think away your fears). You may find that your unwanted thoughts and fears come up only once in a while (but intensely) or all the time. Don't worry about capturing every moment in this exercise, just give yourself a sample.

TRIGGER/DISTRESS/RESPONSE LOG		
Trigger of the Unwanted Thought	Distress Level (1–10)	Physical or Mental Compulsions

Now that you have a picture of the role your triggers play in daily life, let's build a sample hierarchy. Don't worry about committing to this just because you write some things down. This is simply a way to get a picture in your mind of what you could do to stand up to your unwanted thoughts and feelings. Take the triggers from the log above and rewrite them in the order of their distress level (starting with the lowest) in the first column below. Then use the second column to write what you could do to intentionally practice being with that trigger without compulsions. In the third column, write what you would have to resist in order to make the "response prevention" part of ERP effective. You may notice some gaps in the distress levels. See if you can fill them in by coming up with exposures that you think would create that level of distress.

HIERARCHY BUILDER		
Trigger (lowest to highest)	Exposure (ways to practice connecting with the trigger)	Response Prevention (what you will resist)

As you develop some mastery over your triggers at one point in the hierarchy, you can take a step up to the next rung of the ladder. It is not necessary to completely habituate to (or get over) each step before moving on, only that you have demonstrated an ability to cope with the distress effectively without doing compulsions. Returning to the physical fitness metaphor, it is not necessary for one weight to be *light* before moving to heavier weight, only that you start to find the weight easier to lift.

Many people find that once they have started ERP and worked their way up a few steps, the hierarchy falls apart. What you thought was impossible when you first began becomes much less of an issue. As it turns out, it isn't actually necessary to reach the top of your hierarchy. In fact, once you feel capable, it's helpful to jump around the hierarchy and mix up the difficulty levels. This helps you *generalize* (apply the new learning to more than just one context) and reminds you that you can handle your fears when they're easy, when they're hard, when you expect them, and when they take you by surprise.

Responding to Your Unwanted Thoughts Moment to Moment

Setting up a plan for conquering your anxiety and fear around unwanted thoughts is useful, but you may be thinking, *Yeah, but how am I supposed to respond to unwanted thoughts as they arise?* A simple rule to follow is: Don't play defense! Important: This approach applies only to ego-dystonic thoughts (see chapter 1). Ego-dystonic thoughts are the spam emails slipping through the algorithm, and we don't want to be opening those up and replying to them. Ego-*syntonic* thoughts, however, especially those that can lead to harmful behaviors, should be corrected and challenged (more on this in future chapters).

So what does it mean to not play defense with your ego-dystonic unwanted thoughts? It means you have four possible ways to respond that can help you disengage from the thought without doing compulsions:

1. **Ignore it.** You ignore the coupon for Bed Bath & Beyond that shows up in your mailbox, so you can ignore this trash, too. While literally pretending you didn't notice the thought isn't a cure (otherwise, who would need support here?), it is still a perfectly viable option.

2. **Mentally note it.** You can acknowledge, "Oh, hey, there's that thought" without responding to the content of the thought like it's problematic or even interesting.

3. **Casually agree with its uncertainty.** You could say, "Yeah, maybe, I dunno" to the thought content and then immediately return your attention back to wherever it was before the unwanted thought distracted you.

4. **Agree with the thought with *attitude*, using exaggeration, sarcasm, and humor.** You could say, "Oh, yeah, that and then some!" Have fun with the thought. It's taunting you, so taunt it back, but bigger.

Take a moment to consider how you might use these nondefensive responses with your unwanted ego-dystonic thoughts. Don't worry about which is best. Choosing them at random can keep any individual response from getting too repetitive and ritualistic.

Checking In

In this chapter, we described the fundamentals of how to engage in CBT and ERP to develop mastery over your unwanted thoughts. We looked at three ways to approach exposures (in vivo, imaginal, and interoceptive) and five categories of responses/rituals to prevent yourself from doing (avoidance, reassurance, accommodation, neutralizing behaviors, and rumination) so that new learning can take place.

Although ERP is the best way to overcome your fears and learn that you can handle uncertainty, it can be inherently activating and dysregulating. Most change is this way, even good change. It starts with discomfort and stress, then becomes something of value. But when the discomfort and stress of learning something new become overwhelming, we need additional tools to maintain a wise-minded approach to mental health. For this, we have DBT.

CHAPTER 4

The Fundamentals of DBT for Intense Emotions

Under the umbrella of CBT is another powerful treatment approach: dialectical behavior therapy. DBT was originally developed by Dr. Marsha Linehan for the treatment of people who struggle with self-destructive and suicidal behavior, and it subsequently became the gold-standard treatment for BPD. It appeals to many therapists and patients not only because of its effectiveness, but because it integrates four essential elements into one comprehensive treatment approach: the biological, environmental, spiritual, and behavioral aspects of a person's struggle. It's also unique in its focus on balancing the need for a person to change while still completely accepting who they are in the present moment.

What's So Special About DBT?

Broadly speaking, just like ERP, DBT is a type of cognitive behavioral therapy. CBT tries to identify and change negative thinking patterns and pushes for more adaptive and healthy behavioral changes.

In DBT, the term "dialectical" is the concept that seemingly polar opposites can coexist. For instance, you may be exhausted and want to sleep but still get up and go to work. Both wanting to sleep and finding the energy to go to work are existing in the same moment. The central dialectic in DBT is that acceptance of things as they are in the present moment can coexist with the fact that they will change. You might be happy that you have worked hard in therapy and note that you are feeling better overall, and yet you're also sad in the moment because of some struggle in your life. The reality might be that you are suffering with something in the moment, yet it might also be true that you're not dwelling in the suffering but, rather, are rallying to do things to make you more skillful and effective.

The Pillars of DBT

DBT stands on three fundamental pillars that construct the treatment:

1. **All things are interconnected.** Everything and everyone are interconnected and interdependent. We are all part of the greater tapestry of all things, an assemblage of beings that supports and sustains us. We are also connected to our family, friends, and community. We need others and others need us.

2. **Change is constant and inevitable.** This idea is not new—2,500 years ago, the philosopher Heraclitus said, "The only constant in life is change." Life is full of joy, sadness, healing, and suffering, but because change happens, all of these will change, including suffering. Sometimes things change for the better and sometimes for the worse, but if you ever find yourself thinking *This is never going to change*, it simply isn't true, because nothing ever stays the same, and if you behave skillfully, you are likely to suffer less.

3. **Opposites can be integrated to form a closer approximation of the truth.** This tenet lies at the core of dialectics. DBT aims to have a more complete way of seeing yourself and the world. Central to DBT is recognizing that your biology and past experiences may have caused you to struggle, but at the same time, you can change your behavior and choices in order to live more effectively.

Myths About DBT

DBT can seem confusing, and despite the fact that it has the best evidence base for people who struggle with overwhelming emotions, there are a number of myths about it that we should address (just like we did for ERP in the previous chapter).

One myth is that DBT is used only for people with borderline personality disorder. The truth is that extensive research shows that DBT is helpful for many conditions other than BPD, including eating disorders and depression, and as a co-treatment in such conditions as bipolar disorder, PTSD, and substance abuse. We advocate applying many DBT tools alongside ERP for OCD and related anxiety-based conditions as well.

Another myth is that if no other therapy has previously helped, then DBT won't help either. But many people who have struggled with other therapies find success in DBT, typically because many therapies aren't designed to teach skills to people who have emotion regulation problems. DBT recognizes that simply having insight into problems doesn't change the problems. For instance, many people have the insight that eating too many calories is unhealthy and yet they continue to eat excessively. DBT combines awareness of skill deficits with the teaching, implementation, and application of new skills to life's problems.

Yet another myth is that DBT is a form of Buddhism. This misconception comes from the fact that the developer of DBT, Marsha Linehan, formed her mindfulness practices from her experiences with Christian and Buddhist meditation. Mindfulness meditation is common to both secular and religious practice. The reason DBT practices mindfulness skills is to train the brain to pay attention to emotional states so it can apply more effective solutions and attend to ineffective outcomes.

Stages and Format of DBT Treatment

DBT was developed for people with more than just one problem. Many people have complicated lives, challenging relationships, occupational difficulties, and mental health issues. Trying to tackle all of these at once is more than any individual person can manage, so DBT offers a hierarchy of treatment stages that focus on issues that need to be addressed before moving on to the next:

Stage 1: This stage focuses on the individual's most self-destructive behavior, such as suicide attempts, self-injury, and issues that prevent them from showing up to therapy. The idea here is that if you're behaving in self-destructive ways or not showing up to therapy, then therapy is not likely to be helpful. This stage also focuses on behaviors that interfere with quality of life and addresses mental health conditions such as depression and OCD.

Stage 2: This stage of treatment aims to reduce any trauma-related symptoms caused by PTSD and by other traumatic emotional experiences (even if they don't meet the criteria for a formal diagnosis of PTSD).

Stage 3: The task here is to learn to live in a world beyond mental health challenges. It concentrates on defining life goals, building self-worth, and finding peace and happiness.

Stage 4: Finally, DBT aims to create a life that is meaningful for the individual by prioritizing joy and significant relationships.

Even though these stages form the structure of DBT, the end goal is always to create a life worth living, so it's not that stage 4 elements aren't brought into stage 1, only that the predominant focus of stage 1 is the reduction of suffering.

Does DBT Work?

The American Psychiatric Association has recognized DBT as an effective treatment for conditions that involve volatile emotions (like BPD). Research shows that people in DBT treatment note such improvements as:

- Less frequent and less severe suicidal and self-destructive behavior

- Shorter lengths of stay in the hospital

- Less intense and fewer episodes of anger

- Less likelihood of dropping out of treatment

- Improved social and relationship functioning

A full description of DBT for someone undergoing this type of therapy would take up an entire book of its own, so here, we'll only review some of the main elements and points most pertinent for our purposes in this book. Briefly, then, a comprehensive DBT treatment plan would include:

- **Individual therapy:** Similar to many types of psychotherapy, you meet with your therapist regularly to review concerns; however, the difference with DBT is that the sessions focus on the issues described above in the treatment stages, attending to the emotions and behaviors that lead to suffering and then asking you to use new skills to change the course and experience of this suffering.

- **Group skills training:** DBT theory is based on the idea that if you could do things differently, you would, and that the reason you don't is either because you don't know how or that strong emotions get in the way of being more skillful. No one wants to struggle, and so why would you choose not to be more effective? In group training, you are taught DBT skills in a classroom-like setting. New skills are presented and then homework is assigned and reviewed during the next week's group training.

- **Phone coaching:** DBT recognizes that life's problems aren't limited to your weekly three o'clock therapy session on Tuesdays. Because challenges will arise when they do—late at night on a Saturday or during a friend's wedding—and because the point of therapy is to be able to be skillful when you need to be skillful, phone sessions are available. They usually last five to ten minutes, with your therapist giving you immediate support in real time instead of waiting for your next appointment.

- **Consultation team:** Your therapist will belong to larger team of colleagues if they need support or want to brainstorm new ideas that could benefit you.

What Are the Skills DBT Teaches?

Comprehensive DBT focuses on teaching four skill sets to help you deal with overwhelming emotions, volatile relationships, a disturbed sense of self, and unhelpful ways of thinking and behaving. Again, because this isn't a comprehensive DBT book, we'll summarize the ways in which these skills help people who are experiencing difficult-to-control emotions.

Skill Set 1: Mindfulness

Mindfulness is the core skill of DBT. It is "core" because it is central to the other skills. Mindfulness emphasizes the need to be fully present and aware as a first step in using the other skills. It highlights how striving to be less judgmental can make you more compassionate toward yourself and others.

In developing DBT, Linehan wanted a clear way to talk to people about different states of mind, so she came up with: rational mind, emotion mind, and wise mind.

Emotion Mind: Think of emotion mind as the state of thinking and acting driven primarily by your current emotional state. In this state, emotions, rather than facts and logic, drive decision making. There is a time and place for emotion mind, and it can be very useful. But it can nevertheless get a bad rap, sometimes deservedly so. For instance, imagine asking your boss for a raise, then becoming very angry when they suggest that if you can show an increase in productivity, they'll consider it. Not a good idea to act in this state, right? On the flip side, emotion mind can be just what the situation calls for. At a romantic dinner, do you want to spend time calculating the cost of the meal, or would you rather attentively listen to your companion and enjoy your shared timed together?

To determine if you are acting from emotion mind, ask yourself: *Is my behavior dependent on my mood? Do I only get things done if I'm in a good mood, whereas I can't get things done in a bad mood?* Mental health and effective functioning mean doing what needs to be done, independent of mood.

PRACTICE: If you tend to have mood-dependent behavior, we want you to become very aware of this and, further, to notice if and how your response changes depending on your mood. Do you react differently if you are happy, afraid, sad, or angry? Consider some common circumstances:

- Having a fight with a colleague, classmate, or relative

- Skipping work on an impulse without letting your employer know

- Cuddling a puppy or a kitten

- Making love to your partner

- Offering to make dinner for a friend

- Yelling at a driver who just cut you off in a parking lot

- Buying a new pair of shoes, on credit, before paying your rent

- Running away from a barking dog

Now, for each of these circumstances (or for a few that speak more directly to your life), complete this thought process:

When I am in a positive state of mind in this situation, my feelings include: _____

_____

And my behaviors include: _____

_____

But when I am in a negative state of mind in this situation, my feelings include: _____

_____

And my behaviors include: _____

_____

_____

The goal here is to clarify how you respond to events based on your mood. So feel free to use a separate piece of paper to complete this exercise for any number of circumstances you'd like to explore.

Rational Mind: This is a state of mind in which you make decisions based solely on logic and facts. Facts are the parts of a situation that can be observed by you and others. In this state, there is little place for emotions. Say you've had a long day at work and need to buy groceries. Your favorite grocer, with your favorite food items (especially the pizza you're craving for dinner), is thirty minutes from work, in the opposite direction from home, which would add an hour to your commute home, not including the time shopping. Ordinarily, it's worth it to you to make the trip, but you've got an early meeting tomorrow morning. There's a grocer five minutes from work, on your way home. You're not crazy about their food choices, but they'll do in a pinch. The logical decision is to go the grocer closer to you (no matter how much you want that pizza!).

Rational mind has both benefits and downsides. It is helpful in situations where you need to be objective, show forethought, and not let "your emotions get the best of you." Some examples:

- Calling the movie theater ahead of time to see if the new blockbuster is already sold out instead of simply showing up and hoping

- Getting coverage for your shift at work so you can visit a sick friend

- Precisely following a recipe rather than guessing amounts

- Studying for a math test

Now you list some examples applicable to your own life when it makes sense to be driven by logic:

_____

_____

_____

_____

Rational mind is not useful, however, when being informed by your emotions *is* appropriate and acceptable. Say you're at a funeral where everyone is crying and you come out with, "Well, Uncle Joe was eighty-nine, his cholesterol and blood pressure were off the charts, and he wasn't even able to chew his food near the end." All these statements may be completely logical and true, but rational mind is not the state needed in this moment. Nor is it beneficial when:

- A friend who lost their job calls looking for support

- A child petrified by a nightmare needs comfort

- Your partner is very hurt or disappointed by something you've done

Your turn again. Name some situations in your daily life when it's not helpful for you to be in a rational state of mind:

_____

_____

_____

Wise Mind: One way to think about wise mind is to see it as the coming together of rational mind and emotion mind. However, it is more than just that. It is a state that includes both of these elements but is also reflective, contemplative, and intuitive—one less likely to act on impulse. Wise mind seems to emanate from the entire body, leaving you feeling settled, even if there is emotion attached to the decision you have to make.

Let's circle back to the child having a nightmare as an example. You certainly don't want to burst into the room impatiently, scolding your child for ruining your sleep, right? Instead, there's a place for emotion mind here—to hug the child, reassure them that it was just a dream, to listen to their fears and console their tears. There's also room for rational mind: showing the child there's no monster in the closet or under the bed, reminding them that the spooky story they read before bed likely put scary thoughts in their mind. When you integrate emotion with logic, you greatly improve the chances that both you and your child will rest easily for the remainder of the night, both at peace after your encounter.

PRACTICE: Now that you're aware of these three states of mind, reflect on the last few days and write down a few situations in which you can identify the state of mind you were in. As you do so, think about the clues and behaviors leading you to define that state of mind, the different response behaviors you use in each state of mind, and which state of mind serves you best in different situations.

Situation 1: _____

    State of mind: _____

Situation 2: _____

    State of mind: _____

Situation 3: _____

    State of mind: _____

How Does Mindfulness Help with DBT?

DBT emphasizes that accepting reality is the first step in changing behaviors. However, in order to accept reality, you first have to notice it and then describe it as it is, and that is where mindfulness comes in. One of the more difficult aspects to mindfulness is to observe reality without judging it.

When teaching her patients mindfulness skills, Dr. Linehan realized the need to differentiate between *what* to do to practice mindfulness and *how* to do it.

What to Do to Practice Mindfulness

Observe: This is the intentional practice of noticing with your senses, noticing phenomena both inside and outside of yourself. For instance, you might notice an itch, a thought, or an emotion, or you might observe a passing cloud, the sound of a bird, the smell of a cake.

PRACTICE: Sit still for a few minutes and close your eyes. Use your sense of hearing to notice sounds in your environment. After a few minutes, switch your attention to body sensations such as muscle tension and itches. After you have completed these tasks, write down what you noticed:

_____

_____

Describe: This is the intentional practice of putting into words the thing you have observed, describing the sensation of the itch or the content of your thought or the expression of your emotion. You can describe the movement of the cloud, the quality of the birdsong, or the specific aromas of the cake. You might realize that although we have words for so many things and they are the best tool we have to express observations, they don't wholly capture the completeness of an experience. The way you fall in love or see the color blue is not necessarily the way another person experiences those events.

PRACTICE: If you have a pet, observe your pet doing what it does and describe its actions. Put words to your observation: "My dog is playing with a yellow ball," "My cat is wearing a velvet collar," and so on. Notice if your mind wanders to judgment. For instance, the ball is yellow, yes; but if your dog has chewed it to the extent that it's lost its bounce, you might think it useless. That is a judgment because "useless" is not observable; instead, it is your judgment. To the dog, the ball is useful!

Participate: This is the intentional skill of fully throwing yourself into the activity you're doing. When you are talking to a friend, just do that. When you are drinking a cup of tea, just drink the tea with full awareness. When you are walking in the woods, be fully immersed in the experience of walking and being in nature.

PRACTICE: When speaking to a friend, turn off all devices and fully participate in the discussion. When driving, turn off the radio, put away your phone, and notice the experience of less-distracted driving. When eating a bowl of soup, savor it without doing anything else from start to finish—experience the temperature, aromas, flavors, and sensations on your tongue.

How to Practice Mindfulness

Nonjudgmentally: This is the intentional practice of avoiding judgmental tags like "good" or "bad," "fair" or "unfair," "ugly" or "beautiful." It is not that these words aren't useful, but for the practice of mindfulness, they have the effect of ending the description and reducing the likelihood that curiosity will show up. The other problem with these words is that they express a point of view. An impressionist painting may be inspiring to one person and confounding to another. A steak dinner may be delicious to a carnivore and disgusting to a vegetarian. The loss of a sports game may seem unfair to one team and fair to the other.

PRACTICE: Watch a TV channel the politics of which you don't agree with. Notice the judgments that arise. Write them down:

_____

_____

_____

Are these judgments automatic? Are you agreeing or disagreeing with a person or a statement solely on the basis of political party? Have you ever wondered how a view opposed to yours arose? If this is too sensitive an area, turn to judgments about the behaviors or perspectives of a loved one. Do your judgments stop you from being curious?

One-mindfully: This is the intentional practice of doing just one thing in the moment. The idea of effective multitasking is a myth, contrary to the way the brain works. Put aside things that can be done later and do the one thing that is required in the moment.

PRACTICE: If you have to check your email, close down all other apps and simply check your email. If you go for a walk with your partner, turn off your phone so that you are just walking without being distracted by notifications. If you are reading a book, just read the book. Notice what happens when you do things one-mindfully.

Effectively: This is the intentional skill of focusing on what is effective in the moment. There are many times when we just want to prove that we are right and we give up being effective to prove that. Is your goal to be right at all costs, or do you want to be effective? Ideally, you'd be right *and* effective, but it may be more effective to choose to be effective than to insist on being right.

PRACTICE: Think of a disagreement with a loved one where you know you were right. Is your tendency to always insist on being right? Does this insistence negatively impact your relationship? Can it be effective to let some arguments be without insisting on being right?

Skill Set 2: Distress Tolerance

Many people experience negative emotions as overwhelming and unbearable. Without the ability to tolerate the impact of these emotions, you can become overwhelmed by relatively mild levels of stress. If this happens to you, what behaviors (both helpful and unhelpful) do you engage in to deal with the stress?

List a few adaptive, or helpful, behaviors and activities you engage in when stressed:

_____   _____   _____

Now list a few maladaptive, or less useful and perhaps even harmful, behaviors and activities you engage in when stressed:

_____   _____   _____

The distress tolerance skills of DBT can be used to cope more effectively with stressful moments. Let's start with two quick-acting skills before proceeding on with a few others.

STOP

It would be great if we could simply stop having unwanted thoughts and then engaging in maladaptive behaviors in response to them, but we know that changing patterns is difficult. So this skill is a way to slow down and be more effective. STOP is an acronym for: stop, take a step back, observe, and proceed mindfully. More specifically:

Step 1: Literally stop from doing any action. If you are in emotion mind and have an urge to respond strongly, don't.

Step 2: Take a step back. Give yourself some time to get into the state of wise mind—this is an opportunity to slow down and take a breath before responding. For instance, if you want to send an angry text or respond emotionally to an email, pause and take a series of deep breaths while refraining from using your phone or computer.

Step 3: Observe and notice. Objectively assess the facts of the situation, consider alternative interpretations of difficult interactions, and label thoughts as thoughts and emotions as emotions. Furthermore, in this space, notice any judgments you may have about the situation.

Step 4: Proceed mindfully. Once you have slowed down and reflected on the situation and how you're reacting to it with thoughts, urges, and emotions, consider what a wise response would be, based on your long-term goals and values. It may turn out that it is indeed wisest to send that text or email, or perhaps it's better to do nothing in the moment.

TIPP

TIPP is another acronym that represents a set of four activities intended to quickly change your body's physiology so you can change the way your mind interprets thoughts and emotions. When you are in significant distress, try employing the TIPP skill:

T – Temperature: When you are very upset, your heart is racing. To counteract this, start by filling a large bowl with ice cubes and cold water. Take a deep breath, put your face in the water, and hold for thirty seconds. This activates the *mammalian dive reflex*, which is a natural reflex that occurs in all mammals when the face is submerged in cold water. It automatically lowers the heart rate and, in so doing, sends a message to the brain that your emotions are not as intense as you perceive them to be. If need be, repeat this several times. It's not going to take away your emotion, but it will lower the intensity long enough to allow you to make a better choice in the moment (like employing the STOP skill). (A word of caution: If you have a significant heart or respiratory condition, speak to your doctor before trying this technique.)

I – Intense Exercise: This is a great activity to counter the effects of unwanted thoughts. The idea is to engage in an explosive burst of exercise—bursts of sprinting while jogging, holding a plank, lifting weights—until you simply can't do it any longer and are left gasping for air. The intrusiveness of unwanted thoughts diminishes significantly while you are occupied by intense exercise.

P – Paced Breathing: This can be a great skill to use when you notice anxiety. The goal is to slow down your breathing. Take a slow breath in through your nose to the count of four or five seconds, then breathe out even more slowly, to the count of, say, seven or eight seconds. Don't get stuck on the exact number of breaths—the point is to exhale slower than you inhale. You don't even have to count; you can instead say to yourself, *I breathe in slowly to get calm,* and then, *I breathe out even slower to stay calm.* Practice this type of breathing for about two minutes.

P – Paired Muscle Relaxation: This practice is most effective in combination with paced breathing. As you breathe in, tense all the muscles in your body; as you breathe out, relax your muscles. Notice how that feels. Alternately, you can practice progressive muscle relaxation, whereby you choose only one set of muscles at a time—say, your thighs or biceps—tensing them for a few seconds on the inhale, then relaxing them on the exhale. You can progress from one muscle set to another, zeroing in on particular parts of your body as you practice paced breathing.

Radical Acceptance

This third distress tolerance skill is very powerful. It is the practice of experiencing and accepting the reality of any situation exactly as it is, whether you like it or not, even when it is something you cannot change. By practicing radical acceptance without being judgmental, you are more likely to be more skillful and less vulnerable to intense and prolonged negative feelings. Included in radical acceptance is the willingness to accept that this is the situation and then to effectively do what the situation needs.

PRACTICE: Write down a situation you are having a difficult time accepting:

_____

When you refuse to accept the reality of that situation, what emotions show up and what behaviors do you turn to?

_____

_____

Are these consistent with your long-term goals and values? Now write down what accepting the situation as it is would be like:

_____

_____

If you were to stop fighting the reality of your current situation, what would show up? Do you notice a difference between refusing to accept reality and accepting reality?

Additional Distress Tolerance Skills

In addition to the above distress tolerance skills, there are others you can use for temporary relief or to avoid making your situation worse. Think about a situation that is causing you distress right now. With that situation in your mind, consider how applying any of these skill options could help:

- *Distracting yourself.* Can you distract yourself from thinking about the situation by engaging in more neutral or pleasant activities (for example, hobbies, exercises, visiting with friends) rather than ruminating on the distressful situation?

  To distract yourself from the distressing situation, you can: _____

- *Diverting your attention.* Diverting your attention means to refocus your brain away from negative thoughts via such means as puzzles, word games, or counting games.

  For diversion, you can: _____

- *Contributing or volunteering.* Can you "get out of your head" by making a difference for others instead of letting your brain stay mired in your own difficulties?

  You can: _____

- *Eliciting different emotions.* Can you steer yourself away from feeling down and lethargic by doing things to purposely evoke happier emotions (such as watching funny videos or breaking out into song or dance)?

  You can: _____

- *Using strong sensations.* It can be very effective to get through a difficult moment by introducing a pleasant scent or taste to actively engage your senses (like taking a bubble bath).

  You can: _____

- *Improving the situation.* Can you improve the situation you're in? The answer is almost always "yes." How?

  You can: _____

- *Using imagery.* Visualizing a relaxing scene or imagining a successful interaction with a person with whom you are in conflict is a distress tolerance option.

  You can: _____

- *Creating meaning or purpose.* Think about ways in which the stressful situation might actually be of help to you by creating meaning or purpose in your life. In other words, can you devise a silver lining to your situation?

  You can: _____

- *Praying.* For some people, prayer to a higher power can reduce their stress. If this option speaks to you, how can you incorporate it to deal with the situation?

  You can: _____

- *Practicing relaxation.* Can you engage in some form of relaxation to ease the tension of the situation (deep breathing, taking a warm bath, doing gentle yoga or stretching)?

  You can: _____

Create a list of pros and cons

Lastly, you can take advantage of this tool to analyze the situation from different angles: the pros and cons of tolerating the distress and the pros and cons of not tolerating the stress. When creating such a list, it is useful to keep in mind the past consequences of not having tolerated the distress while also imaging how it will feel to successfully tolerate the current distress and avoid unhelpful behaviors. You also want to make your list with your long-term goals and values in mind.

Write down a situation causing you distress: _____

What is your long-term goal in alleviating this distress? _____

Pros of Tolerating Your Distress	Cons of Tolerating Your Distress

Pros of Not Tolerating Your Distress	Cons of Not Tolerating Your Distress

Based on these lists and given your long-term goal here, your action plan to better tolerate this distressing situation is:

_____

_____

_____

Skill Set 3: Interpersonal Effectiveness

Interpersonal effectiveness skills aim to build and maintain positive relationships. Often, strong emotional responses can negatively impact your relationships. If you've noticed that this is the case for you, here are some ideas that can help. As we proceed through this section, you'll likely have an important relationship in mind, so think about how it has been impacted by your difficult-to-control emotions as we concentrate on three goals: (1) obtaining your objectives; (2) maintaining healthy relationships; and (3) maintaining your self-respect.

Obtaining Your Objectives

It can be hard not to get what you want, especially if you feel entitled to it; and sometimes, when you are blocked from getting what you want, this can lead to strong emotions that worsen relationships and decrease the likelihood of getting what you're looking for.

Write down a situation in which you are asking someone for something you feel is reasonable:

_____

In this situation, your objective is: _____

Let's say someone's objective is to get a raise at work. It may feel satisfying in the short term to barge into the boss's office and bark out the reasons why a raise is deserved, but is that behavior likely to secure the raise? Or imagine yelling at your parents because you feel you don't get the same treatment from them that your siblings do—is putting them on the defensive likely to be effective or improve your relationships with them?

There is a skillful approach you can take to stay calm while you work to meet your objective in any scenario:

- Explain the facts of the situation ("Boss, I have been in my job for three years").

- Express how you feel about it ("I like my job and feel I have significantly contributed to the company by so-and-so").

- Assert clearly what you are asking for ("I'm asking for a 10 percent raise on the basis of these accomplishments").

- Consider what's in it for the other person to agree to your objective. (Note: This is likely the most important step in this approach!) For example, "By giving me the raise, I will continue to increase productivity, feel more loyal to the company, and would be willing to train other employees."

While practicing this skill, stay mindful of what you are asking for, be confident in knowing that your request is valid, and, finally, be prepared to negotiate if your objective can't be fully met (for instance, settling for an 8 percent raise).

PRACTICE: How can you use this skill to address the objective you identified above? On a separate piece of paper or on your computer, write out the facts of that situation, your feelings about it, specifically what you're looking to achieve, and why it would also benefit the other person in your action plan.

Maintaining Healthy Relationships

If a relationship has been rocky, there can be enduring tension in the air that can lead to distancing, made worse by strong emotions. Are you in a situation with someone you care about that is being impacted by distancing based on your strong emotions?

If so, the skillful way to go about improving the health of your relationships is to avoid personal attacks of all kinds; instead, try to approach the situation with empathy and compassion, recognizing that the other person has feelings in this situation with you as well. Try being (or at least acting like you are) interested in their point of view and validating their perspective. Then gently clear the air, reinforce that the relationship is important to you, and clarify that your goal is to have a more effective way of interacting in the event of future conflict.

Maintaining Your Self-Respect

If you don't like yourself, feel worthless, or feel irrelevant, you might do things that aren't consistent with your values, instead thinking you deserve it if bad things happen to you. We strongly challenge that idea. The worth of every person is equal, and you have an equal right to maintain your self-respect. If what you're doing in any given relationship isn't right for you, then, ultimately, it isn't right for the other person either. Don't be a "people pleaser" at the cost of your self-respect.

Here's a way to approach protecting your self-respect in challenging relationships:

1. Do you have a relationship in which you do things that don't honor your own worth and values?

    Write it down: _____

2. What values are you not upholding in your interactions with this person?

    _____

3. What would be right for you—would maintain your self-respect—in this relationship?

    _____

    _____

4. What would be right for the other person, would maintain their rights and self-respect as well?

    _____

    _____

5. Stick to the values you identified in step 2—you never need to apologize for having the values and perspective that you have.

6. Finally, tell the truth. Don't lie or make excuses. Doing so, in fact, will keep you trapped in an unhealthy relationship with this person, because you are not honoring your own truth.

Skill Set 4: Emotion Regulation

Finally, we get to the DBT skill module of emotion regulation—the primary focus of this book on unwanted thoughts and intense emotion. We introduced the other DBT skills first, though, because strong emotions don't impact only your emotional health; they also affect your relational health, your behaviors, the way you think, and your sense of self.

How long do you think an emotion lasts in the brain? Believe it or not, brain scientists have found that the electrical and chemical event that equates to an emotion lasts fewer than ninety seconds. But it feels to us like an emotion lasts longer than a minute and a half because we tend to enhance our emotions by fueling them with repetitive and often unhelpful thoughts and ruminations. But there are DBT skills you can use to transform your emotions over time. These involve paying attention to the behaviors and factors that increase unwanted thoughts and emotions and then practicing effective strategies to decrease those behaviors and factors instead. More specifically, because emotion regulation skills of DBT focus on the building blocks of long-term emotional health, you want to regularly do things that improve your mood, prepare for difficult situations that impair your mood, and attend to the vulnerability factors that can lead to prolonged emotion mind.

Before we cover these skills in more detail, compose a few lists to keep in mind as we discuss ways to regulate your emotions:

Five Behaviors That Bring You Joy	Five Behaviors That Keep You Stuck or Make Things Worse

When you are feeling down, do you tend to give up the behaviors in the first list or engage in the behaviors in the second list?

Improving Your Mood

You can improve mood by regularly engaging in activities that have historically made you happy. Often, when people are depressed, they give up the things that make them happy and keep doing the things that keep them depressed. Look at your list of behaviors that bring you joy. Are you not only doing them in your life, but doing them regularly? If not, what is getting in the way of doing them?

Another way to enhance your mood is to build mastery in these behavior areas; for example, if listening to music is one of the ways you find joy, might you perhaps take music lessons to further your enjoyment of this activity? If cooking is one of your passions, would you be interested in taking culinary courses to extend your mastery here?

Coping Ahead

Another way to regulate emotions is to plan ahead for difficult situations—we call this *coping ahead*. If you can anticipate situations that elicit intense negative emotions (such as a visit from a parent), cope-ahead skills allow you to prepare for things that can go wrong. The idea is to have a plan in place for when unwanted outcomes seem likely and then to rehearse that plan over and over, perhaps role-playing the expected situation with a friend. If the situation doesn't arise, great; but if does, you'll be ready for it.

What you're doing here is replacing rumination on the "what ifs" with a strategy to handle them if they actually happen. Note that coping ahead can also apply to OCD and similar conditions: you devise a plan for how to resist or limit compulsions at an upcoming event, then you implement that plan when and if triggers arise at the event.

PRACTICE: Write down an upcoming situation you are worried about: _____

Now imagine the least-wanted thing happening at that event and develop a plan to address it. If you can, rehearse your plan with someone you trust.

Addressing Vulnerability Factors

If negative emotions are interfering with the positives in your life, it's time to look at reducing the vulnerability factors that lead to those emotions enduring rather than lessening.

Physical illness. One of the most common vulnerability factors is physical illness. If you have a medical condition like migraines, sinus infections, diabetes, or high blood pressure, it can make emotion regulation more challenging. To help mitigate the challenge, you can be more attentive to your physical health.

If you have a health care issue, write it down here: _____

The phone number for the doctor treating this issue for you is: _____

Commit to making an appointment with this doctor to go over your concerns by this date: _____

Screen time. The next common vulnerability factor is screen time. Excessive amounts can worsen the quality of sleep, and spending time on social media apps can lead to emotional distress for some people.

How much time are you are spending on-screen? _____

Will you consider adding a tracking app to your devices to tally your screen time? _____

If certain apps make you feel worse about yourself, why do you continue to use them?

_____

_____

Food. Another vulnerability factor is our relationship with food. We may eat too much or too little; we may fall prey to being hangry—being angry or irritable when hungry. But attending to food goes beyond just quantity and the way certain foods make us feel. The skill here is to be mindful of when, what, and how much you eat; the impact that has on your mood; and, further, what foods to stay away from if you know they make you feel grouchy. What we feed ourselves on the inside does indeed affect what comes out on the outside.

Drugs. We also want you to pay attention to the impact any drugs you are taking (whether prescribed or not) have on your mood. Just because a drug does not impact a friend's mood doesn't mean it won't impact yours. Be aware of what various chemicals do to you. If a prescription medication is negatively impacting your mood, talk to your prescriber about changing it.

If a particular substance impacts your mood, write the substance down here: _____

When you take this drug, the short-term effect is: _____

And the long-term effect is: _____

Sleep. We're not always aware of the impact of sleep on our mood, yet few of us are at our emotional best without adequate sleep. If sleep is an issue for you, consider the elements you *can* control, such as what time you go to bed, whether there's too much light in the room or too many devices keeping you up, the temperature of the room, and whether you've eaten or ingested a substance before going to bed. Make modifications to these elements and see if your sleep quality improves; if not, you might want to speak to your health care provider about a sleep aid that could help.

If you are not getting quality sleep, record the impact on you:

When I sleep too little, I feel _____

When I sleep too much, I feel _____

Exercise. Finally, the importance of regular exercise on emotion regulation cannot be overstated. Research has proven the beneficial role of regular exercise on all aspects of health, and yet many people feel they don't have time to add it to their daily routine. Even small changes can help, such as parking your car farther away in parking lots so you can walk a little more or taking the stairs rather than the elevator.

Opposite Action

There's one last important emotion regulation skill within DBT that we want to discuss with you: *opposite action* or *different action*. Here's how it works: when a strong emotion is activating you to do something unhelpful or ineffective, do the opposite instead. This might sound similar to ERP in that both approaches ask you to practice something different from what you have been conditioned to do and to believe. When you're feeling sad, for instance, your pattern might be to isolate, stay in bed, and not exercise. Opposite action advises you to get out and be with other people and push yourself to be active. The idea is to counter an unhelpful habit with something more helpful to you.

One caveat, though: If the emotion or impulse is justified—that is, if it fits the facts—*don't* do the opposite action. For example, if you are standing on train tracks and a train is approaching, fear is justified and you should bolt off the tracks. If, on the other hand, you are avoiding applying for a job you want and are qualified for out of fear of rejection, then your fear is unjustified and you can engage in the opposite action of, indeed, completing the application.

Let's come up with a few different opposite actions to apply to your daily life, following the same formula for each—filling in an emotion, your regular behavior in response to that emotion, and then an opposite behavior you can try instead:

When I feel _____, I tend to _____.

Instead, I can _____.

When I feel _____, I tend to _____.

Instead, I can _____.

When I feel _____, I tend to _____.

Instead, I can _____.

Checking In

Now that you have a broad overview of various ERP and DBT skills, we recommend that you return to these last two chapters as often as needed until the skills become second nature. We covered quite a lot in this one, including the four core skills of DBT (mindfulness, distress tolerance, interpersonal effectiveness, and emotion regulation) and several individual skills within them (such as STOP, TIPP, and opposite action). Hopefully, you now have a solid sense of what ERP and DBT are all about. The next step is to tie them both together.

CHAPTER 5

ERP and DBT Together

It may seem like ERP and DBT are sometimes coming from opposite perspectives. ERP intentionally increases contact with unwanted thoughts and feelings, while DBT intentionally decreases intensity around thoughts and feelings. In truth, both approaches complement each other quite well because they have the same end goal: to reduce unnecessary suffering caused by unwanted thoughts and emotional overwhelm. They both use your ability to learn from changing your behavior and your perspective to make you more effective in navigating life's challenges. Although ERP may be more commonly associated with overcoming unwanted thoughts and reducing compulsive behavior, and DBT may be more commonly associated with navigating difficult emotions and making wise decisions, these two forms of cognitive behavioral therapy share some important core concepts.

Mindfulness

Positioning oneself as the observer of consciousness, being one who *witnesses* thoughts and feelings arising as opposed to being one who identifies with or is fused to those thoughts and feelings—this is at the root of the concept of mindfulness. At any given moment, you are either aware/awake or unaware/lost in stories. Mindfulness is the ability to distinguish between what you are experiencing right now and the state of being carried away by mental narratives.

You can easily be a witness to this right now by simply bringing your attention to your feet. Point your mind to the sensations in the bottom of your feet. What do you notice? Pressure, perhaps? Tingling? Maybe no sensation at all? Well done—you just connected with an experience.

Now take a moment to wonder about this book and whether its contents are really going to help you. Wonder about whether there may be something wrong with the book that doesn't make it a good fit for you. Wonder about whether there may be something wrong with you that makes you less receptive to the ideas herein. Wonder or *wander* around your mind looking for answers. Take your time.

Okay, now come back to these words right in front of you. Did you notice a difference between the *experience* of observing your feet and the *story* in your head when you were wandering aimlessly in your mind in response to our prompts? Noticing that difference is the key to mindfulness. Meditation (and a wide variety of meditative practices) is simply practicing this awareness by discovering when we are lost in a story and returning our attention to present-moment experience.

Mindfulness necessarily involves ERP, just as ERP necessarily involves mindfulness. This may not be instinctively obvious since people will sometimes say they "do" exposure *or* they "do" mindfulness when dealing with unwanted thoughts and feelings. But, in fact, becoming aware of an intrusive thought (*What if I'm a bad parent? What if I have a disease? What if I accidentally harmed someone?*) and then returning your attention to present-moment experience without first doing compulsions is quite an exposure! What if you were supposed to really sit and stew on your unwanted thought, figure it out and guarantee that your fears are untrue? And what if you then just noticed the urge to analyze and dropped it? That is impressive and scary exposure therapy.

We may associate the word "mindfulness" with trying to stay calm, but that's only because we are at our most anxious when we are lost in stories, not being mindful. In actuality, mindfulness has little to do with being calm and everything to do with being *present.* If you are engaging in ERP effectively, your number one instruction is to stay present with unwanted thoughts and feelings as they arise and witness your changing relationship with them over time. As discussed earlier, this change may be habituation (a reduction in distress) or inhibitory learning (a reduction in the pressure to avoid distress). If you attempt ERP without mindfulness, you simply get rumination and despair.

For example, consider using ERP to try to overcome a fear of fecal contamination. An obvious exposure would be touching the outside of a toilet, and an obvious response prevention would be resisting washing your hands. But what happens between the exposure and the response prevention? You feel distressed (anxious, disgusted, dirty, and so on). If you are mindful in this space, you experience the distress and you witness how your relationship to it evolves. If you are not mindful but instead spend that time trying to convince yourself that you won't be harmed by the exposure, figuring out the likelihood of a molecule of feces making its way on to your skin, and fantasizing about when you will get to wash and feel clean again (story, story, and story, by the way), then ERP is unlikely to be effective. All you will have learned is what you already knew: that you don't like feeling that way. In other words, you have to be there for the exposure, not lost in a story.

Again, a mindful relationship to ERP would be to notice the feeling of contamination and allow it. You could also allow in the rest of the experience (the sounds in the room, the temperature of the air on your face, the feeling of your feet against the ground as you walk to your next activity). You can further allow yourself to remain aware of thoughts and feelings about contamination *without* giving them all your attention.

This is where DBT can be very helpful for difficult exposures. The fundamental instruction behind DBT is to step back, take a look at what is really going on in the moment, then plan your next move accordingly. By combining emotion regulation with critical thinking (wise and methodical, *not* self-critical!), DBT is an invitation to show up to the present moment and observe. We get our feelings in a more tolerable and yet still accessible place, and then we can be better observers. We drop out of our stories and stop punishing (or, in some cases, literally harming) ourselves so we can be better observers.

Acceptance of Uncertainty

We're going to assume that you are a person who is often acutely attuned to your unwanted thoughts and feelings and who therefore has to spend quite a bit of time turning away from internal prompts. Imagine someone asking you the same question over and over; at some point, you'd just give up answering and treat them as a distraction to turn away from, right? You probably find yourself noticing and turning away from many thoughts throughout the day. Perhaps you have a primary obsession that's most difficult to let go (like the relentlessly intrusive thought of being responsible for hit-and-run accidents), but you likely also have plenty of *other* random unwanted thoughts that you easily brush off throughout the day. What this suggests is not that you are bad at accepting uncertainty, but that you struggle to apply the concept of uncertainty to your specific obsession.

Every time we have any kind of unwanted thought and choose not to dwell on it, we are fundamentally accepting uncertainty. It may not always *feel* like uncertainty, but it is. As you read this, you are accepting uncertainty that a sinkhole may open below you and swallow you up. Now that this idea has been put in your head, you are literally accepting uncertainty by continuing to read these lines. And it feels easy to keep reading because you don't have an obsession with being swallowed by a sinkhole.

This is another area where you might want to consider mindful awareness of the experience in your body and how it differs from being caught up in your emotions. Accepting uncertainty about the sinkhole is easy because you *feel* safe and you trust that feeling even while thinking about the sinkhole. But in an actual obsession, your feelings may confuse you, trick you into thinking you are unsafe, can't trust your instincts, and must do whatever it takes to get certain that you will not be swallowed up into the earth.

PRACTICE: Take a moment to consider some of the things in life over which you have no issue accepting uncertainty. For example, if you are comfortable driving a car, then you are willing to accept uncertainty that an unanticipated event could cause you to crash the car. If you had a meal recently, you are accepting uncertainty that what you ate might make you sick. Write some examples of your acceptance of uncertainty here:

_____

_____

_____

_____

Compulsions are strategies for reducing distress by trying to get certain about the content of an unwanted thought. For example, you may worry excessively about having hurt someone's feelings, and so even though they already assured you things were fine, you message them again, seeking reassurance. When you get the reply back, *No, I wasn't offended at all—we're all good*, that makes you feel more certain that you didn't do something bad.

Compulsions aim at eliminating unwanted experiences by trying to be sure about them, working *around* uncertainty acceptance where your tolerance may be low. Coping and regulation skills, on the other hand, are aimed at keeping you *in* the experience without dissociating or harming yourself or others. With ERP, we are running experiments to try to learn that we can handle uncertainty, even about really, really disturbing things, and that *thoughts* about disturbing things aren't inherently harmful. When we bring in DBT skills, we are also learning that we can handle uncertainty about our feelings, how long they will last, and how willing we can be to experience them; we learn that *all* feelings are impermanent.

Psychological Flexibility

There's a memorable scene in the classic HBO show *The Wire* in which a particularly cold and calculating criminal is confronted by a security guard after stealing something from a store. The security guard asks the criminal as politely as he can to not be so brazen in his disregard for the law. The criminal responds, "You want it to be one way. But it's the other way." Though the writers probably didn't intend this tense moment to be a lesson in psychological flexibility, the words capture the concept perfectly.

We want things to be one way and sometimes grow to expect them to be one way, and when we discover that they are another way, our instinct is to resist. We become avoidant, frustrated, even willful. *I shouldn't have to have these thoughts and feelings! I should have some other experience than this one!* The tendency is to believe we are in control of what happens in our lives. We think of ourselves as authors of our lives and our lives as our autobiographies. But then when we are faced with unwanted thoughts and feelings, we get reminded that we are not the authors. We are the readers.

In ERP, we intentionally do things that are hard, and we intentionally go in the opposite direction from avoidance, reassurance, and other compulsions. We do this because psychological *inflexibility*, or the difficulty we have pivoting to new skills when faced with triggering thoughts and feelings, lies at the root of suffering. ERP stretches the rigid parts of the mind, and just like stretching at the gym, it can be uncomfortable, but it ultimately reduces more painful injuries from occurring later.

DBT also teaches psychological flexibility. The very concept of a dialectic—two opposing forces occupying the same space—requires psychological flexibility. The simplest way to understand this is to look at the difference between "but" statements and "and" statements. Anyone with a complicated relationship with a parent, partner, or other loved one knows this well. You love the person *but* you are angry with them. Your anger makes it hard to continue feeling as if you love them, because now you have to deal with this anger over something they did or said. Consider what it would be like to mindfully observe that you love this person *and* you are angry with them.

Choice

Compulsions are behavioral decisions. They feel like they have to be done because they are driven by beliefs about ourselves and what we can tolerate. But all compulsions begin with choice and end with choice. Impulsive or otherwise problematic behaviors found in BPD and related disorders may not feel like choices—for example, a sudden and overwhelming urge to punch a wall. Impulsive acts certainly can sneak up on you in the heat of distress. But then intentionally observing the state of impulsiveness and intentionally utilizing skills for reducing that type of distress in a wise-minded way is a choice.

Recall the concept of "wise mind" from chapter 4. Here, by "wise-minded," we mean taking a balanced and thoughtful view of your experience to choose intentionally effective behaviors. DBT identifies four choices for any distressing situation: (1) solve the problem; (2) change your perception of the problem; (3) radically accept the situation; or (4) stay miserable. Staying miserable doesn't sound like much of a choice, but it still is. And then, of course, there's also the option of making the problem worse.

We are not suggesting that resisting compulsions or finding a wise way to navigate painful emotions is easy. In fact, these are the hardest choices we have to make. Someone with obsessive thoughts about harming their child (an OCD symptom new mothers often have) is understandably going to say, "I can't stop worrying about it." This position of not having a choice is the backbone of feeling compelled to engage in all the other compulsions (such as avoidance and reassurance seeking).

In DBT and ERP therapy, we discourage people from saying they "can't" do things that are beneficial or therapeutic (including exposures), and we try to collaborate on ways to get back to "I'm choosing to avoid this because of how it makes me feel." Recall the essential DBT concept that we must first accept the experience before we can get clarity on how to change it.

Genuine Connection

Evidence-based protocols sometimes get a bad rap in the psychotherapy community because, on the surface, they appear to be formulaic. Both ERP and DBT manuals flood the market with good but formulaic step-by-step guides for overcoming what ails you. *Don't look, you're reading one right now!* Both ERP and DBT love worksheets. Fill this out, write this down, then schedule this, plan that, record it, report it, track it, tell your therapist about it, and practice it. But there's a reason why no book (even this one) is a perfect substitute for therapy: because therapy is a relationship. It is a relationship with specific boundaries and inherent agreements that ethically preserve the effectiveness of the therapy process. It is not a friendship in a social context, though at its most effective, it is driven by all the same features of a social friendship (mutual respect, shared interests, the desire for the other to be free of suffering and full of joy). It is not a romantic relationship, though at its most effective, it is characterized by an intimacy, a shared vulnerability, and a genuine love for the other person.

Both ERP and DBT involve storytelling and strategic self-disclosure on the part of the therapist. People with OCD and related disorders often carry around a lot of shame for what they believe are unacceptable or embarrassing thoughts and behaviors. Trust in a therapy relationship is essential for working through this shame and finding the courage to do exposure to what scares you. People with BPD and related disorders have often had their trust or their expectations of people violated. They have often been invalidated because others do not seem to understand why they are so upset or so concerned about being rejected. Knowing they are working with a genuine human being creates an opportunity to experiment with trust in a relationship that is corrective. If you do not have either of these diagnoses but traits from one or both (such as a hard time coping with your thoughts and feelings), all of the above still applies.

You may be reading this without also being in therapy, but the concept of genuine connection still has relevance. In this case, as the self-help reader, you are forming a genuine connection with yourself and allowing the guidance of this book to enhance that.

Self-Compassion

We've previously discussed some myths about ERP and DBT. ERP is often wrongfully associated with torture or self-abuse, as if it were an unkind or dehumanizing form of therapy. DBT is often wrongfully associated with coddling or patronizing people, telling them how to manage basic human experiences and just "normal up" already. But if any one concept brings ERP and DBT together, it's the role of self-compassion, that genuine connection with yourself.

Evidence-based psychotherapies set out to answer one question: What would be helpful? By organizing symptoms and traits into identifiable diagnoses, different groups of people with shared characteristics can report back on whether or not a particular intervention truly reduced their suffering. Even if you do not meet the criteria for the conditions we've been referencing, the combined ERP and DBT tools are helpful for anyone who struggles with thoughts and feelings. Compassion is something that would benefit anyone. Compassion is defined as empathy (being able to feel what others feel) plus the desire to reduce suffering. Empathy without this desire is simply being annoyed all the time by the distress of the people around you. The desire to reduce suffering without empathy is blindly guessing what might help someone without having any real connection to them and what they are experiencing. Witnessing your own pain is being empathic toward yourself. And desiring to reduce your own suffering is to imagine a safer, more joyful version of yourself, then striving for that. Together, they spell self-compassion.

ERP requires self-compassion. Gritting your teeth and white-knuckling through exposures only ever teaches you that you can do hard things by plowing through them, not by actually mastering them. A self-compassionate approach asks you to be present for the exposures, to see the universality in the human experience of distress, and to make the decision to be kind to yourself by resisting behaviors that fuel your painful disorder.

Whereas ERP may involve a kind of tough self-compassion, the kind a good coach offers on a soccer field ("You can do this, now show some hustle!"), DBT offers a kind of protective embrace for when things get out of hand. In other words, when painful emotions get so high that they start to bring on self-hatred and unwise escape plans, DBT skills are there to help you step back and reengage with your wise mind. Rather than align with your OCD by providing reassurance or avoidance, DBT skills applied well can help keep you in the game.

Further, while DBT may be the first tool of choice in helping you care for yourself when your mind is flooded with thoughts of emptiness, confusion, and self-destruction, it doesn't just end there. After all, something escalated you to the point of needing DBT skills, so bringing in thoughtful exposure to *that* is the boldest of self-compassionate strategies.

Seeing Beyond Your Diagnoses

Most people who seek help for mental health challenges have a combination of difficulties with unwanted thoughts and emotion regulation. Self-stigma is often the biggest barrier to looking to ERP and DBT right from the start.

One way to think about the difference between disorders like OCD and BPD is to consider what you really feel like when each condition is manifesting in your life. For most with OCD or a related disorder, the feeling is much like doing something wrong all the time. It's as if everybody knows how to breathe normally, but you somehow can't seem to do it and always feel short of breath. You know you're supposed to be breathing differently to get more oxygen, but you just keep messing it up somehow, and it's exhausting. It's easy to beat yourself up for not knowing how to do something everyone else seems to be doing with ease.

If you also have a personality disorder, such as BPD, you may feel like you are breathing the way any reasonable person would—the only way that makes any sense: inhale and exhale—but the problem is in the air itself. It's like trying to survive on a planet that just doesn't have the right amount of oxygen for your lungs. If only the world could just make the air easier to breathe, you'd be okay. You survive somehow, but it's not fair and it's exhausting.

So what's worse? Believing you can't breathe or believing there isn't enough oxygen? They're both terrifying positions. That's why it's not fair to say that those with personality disorders are complainers while those with other mental health conditions are victims. Both are just qualities of people doing the best they can.

A psychiatric diagnosis like OCD is a biopsychosocial condition. That means you started with a genetic or familial predisposition that was not your fault, and then your attempts to navigate the world with this condition led to learning that your thoughts were dangerous and you'd have to rely on compulsions to survive—also not your fault.

A personality disorder like BPD is a series of traits you develop in response to your experiences, only these traits become too concrete or rigid over time and make it difficult to navigate changes in your environment. For example, having your feelings repeatedly invalidated by people you trust can lead to a very rigid belief that relationships are inherently dangerous and unreliable. Believing that you are doomed to be rejected no matter what can lead to compulsive efforts to get certainty about that in a relationship. This can manifest as pushing people away or creating conflict that facilitates you being rejected, just to get it out of the way already. It can be easy to judge someone who struggles with stability in relationships and just call them "difficult" or use "borderline" as a pejorative, but in reality, these people are just trying to breathe.

Checking In

Well, you've certainly been taking in a lot of information! Don't worry if it all seems like a lot to remember; there won't be a test. What there will be, in the next section, is a collection of stories about people who struggle with unwanted thoughts and intense emotions. Some use ERP first and find DBT helps them achieve success, while others use DBT to get to a place where ERP can bring it all home. Each of them, like you, has to troubleshoot their interventions to find what works best.

Ultimately, if you feel like you're struggling and losing hope, then you may be stuck trying to get one intervention to "work" for you when another intervention may be more effective. Or you may be engaging in the best intervention for you in your context, but missing one or two small but important adjustments that can really make a difference. The next part of this book will help define and clarify these adjustments.

PART TWO

Effective Skills for Complex Experiences

In part 1 of this book, we explored how different kinds of thoughts can lead to painful emotions when they become conditioned to do so. We also explored how different emotions, in turn, shine a light back on those thoughts that led us astray in the first place. Some examples:

- You think you may have touched something with pesticides on it and you begin to worry that you transferred this to your child. You become anxious. But then you tell yourself it's stupid to worry about something so small and unlikely. But then you become ashamed at how anxious you are. So then you begin to criticize yourself for being so weak. But then you still have the worry that you might poison your child. So you avoid your child. And then you hate yourself.

- You have an interaction with a colleague at work that leaves you feeling off. You begin to ruminate over whether or not you said something inappropriate. You begin to feel nervous that you really did. Then you ruminate over why this person makes you nervous and begin to judge them for acting like they're smarter or better than you. Then you begin to feel anger toward them, then toward yourself for being so judgmental. Your anger escalates while you think about how you may be losing your mind and all you want to do right now is put your fist through a wall.

Feedback loops like these play out in similar ways in each of the diagnoses we've been discussing, but also in the nonclinical world. There are many ways thoughts and feelings end up intertwined, but how we think about them and behave around them has a tremendous impact. Thoughts and feelings inform our behavior, but with the right tools, you can strategically modify your behavior to change the way thoughts and feeling impact you. The tools we emphasize for this purpose are cognitive behavioral interventions, especially exposure and response prevention and dialectical behavior therapy.

In the chapters ahead, we will go over a series of common areas of confusion people face when trying to navigate unwanted thoughts and painful emotions at the same time. Those familiar with interventions for dealing with intrusive thoughts and fears may employ cognitive and exposure-based interventions. But those who have difficulty regulating intense internal states (those who find their thoughts and feelings overwhelming) may also benefit from DBT-based interventions. Those more familiar with DBT-style coping strategies may enjoy the benefits of reducing the intensity of self-hatred and emotional chaos, but then find that the problem of unwanted obsessive thoughts still needs to be addressed.

You have good reason to feel frustrated when exposure and DBT strategies seem to be saying different things. Exposure strategies may emphasize letting go of analysis and not trying to figure out if your fears are true before moving on. But DBT strategies may encourage looking at the evidence for and against justification for how you feel about your fears. This part of the book thus aims to clarify where ERP and DBT can achieve the best outcomes together to be most effective. Even if each chapter doesn't apply directly to your own challenges, it can still be useful to explore these concepts to assess how they may help you.

CHAPTER 6

Coping vs. Compulsing

If you are familiar with using ERP to confront your fears, you may already understand that learning to be present with distress without doing compulsions is essential to making progress. This can lead to some confusion, however, around how much distress you should expect to endure and what you are or are not "allowed" to do about it. Sometimes people practicing exposures conflate coping with distress with using compulsions, so let's clarify this even further.

A compulsion is a strategy for escaping uncertainty. It reduces distress specifically by making you feel as if your fears are more certainly untrue. If you have an intrusive thought about your sexuality and ask a loved one for reassurance that you are not attracted to the "wrong" thing, this is a compulsion because it addresses the uncertainty about the content of your fear. Coping, in contrast, doesn't do this, even though it may help soothe your distress. Using the example above, it is *not* compulsive to respond to anxiety around an intrusive sexual thought by taking a slow breath and telling yourself, *Wow, that's uncomfortable. Okay, I can handle this; let's go back to what I was doing before I got triggered.* Notice how this doesn't address the content of the thought or the uncertainty. It simply addresses the distress and allows you to remain with the uncertainty.

Put succinctly, compulsions are about escape and coping is about navigation. Compulsions take you away from the distress by trying to get certain about the content of your unwanted thoughts. Coping strategies allow you to better handle your distress and are unrelated to the content of the intrusive thoughts. Meditation and exercise, for example, may reduce distress, but they are likely to be coping strategies (unless you have a fear of not being mindful or obsessions around fitness).

Here is the experience of Gladys:

Gladys is a twenty-five-year-old woman who recently started her dream job in an accounting firm. She grew up in a small town and went to a small college, but her job is in a major city. Her father is an anxious person and is worried about her living in the city. He repeatedly warns her that she has to make sure she's safe, and his worry increased after she rented an affordable apartment in a part of the city he considers dangerous. Because Gladys has never lived in a city before and wasn't used to locking her door in her small town, she made certain that her apartment was above street level and also installed extra security in the apartment, including a doorbell camera and triple locks on the door.

Soon after moving in, Gladys started to check that the locks were properly bolted. Each time she checks, she tells herself that she has checked and she knows she has checked, but as she turns to leave for the subway, she starts to fear that someone will break in and steal her possessions or that they'll be lying in wait for her upon her return. She worries that if she is not completely certain that the door is locked, it will be her fault if she is robbed or hurt. She struggles to balance her strong compulsive urge to keep checking the locks with the importance of her job, and she also recognizes the need to cope with her distress.

In her efforts to use DBT coping skills—in particular, distress tolerance skills—she gets stuck, feeling that she is caving in to not checking her door and that she will deserve it if something bad happens. Eventually, every morning, she can't tolerate resisting the urge and she turns around and goes back for one last check; she barely gets to work on time, which in turn makes her worry that everyone will think she is terrible employee.

You Don't Have to Comply with Your Unproductive Compulsions

In the world of behavioral treatments, there are several core principles, including:

- Psychological problems are based, in part, on faulty or unhelpful ways of thinking. In Gladys's case, it is the thought or fear that she has left her door unlocked and that terrible things will happen because of it.

- Psychological problems are based, in part, on learned patterns of unhelpful behavior. In this case, Gladys has a history of being told repeatedly that the world is dangerous and that she has to be certain she is safe.

- People suffering from the kinds of problems that Gladys has can learn better ways of coping with difficult situations, thereby relieving their symptoms and living more effectively.

However, there are times when the principles appear to clash. The DBT skills of coping with situations might interfere with the exposure tasks demanded by ERP. The "exposure" part of ERP refers to exposing yourself to the thoughts, fears, and situations that make you anxious and lead you to your compulsions, while the "response prevention" part means making the choice not to engage in the compulsive behavior once the fear or obsession has been triggered. But when fear arises for a person,

DBT would ask: Is this fear justified or unjustified? It is justified if the situation fits the facts and unjustified if it doesn't fit the facts. (Later on, you can follow a step-by-step guide to check the facts.)

When a fear is in fact justified, you avoid the situation. For example, it is justified to be afraid of running across a busy highway because you are likely to get hit by a car, so avoiding running across a highway makes sense. If a fear is not justified, however, DBT would have you say, *My fear is unjustified, and so I need not act on my fear urges to run away or avoid.* In Gladys's case, her fear of leaving her door unlocked is unjustified, so we would advise that she tolerate her distress and resist checking that her door is locked.

In DBT, you lean into the fear if it is unjustified and avoid the situation if it is justified, yet in ERP, you expose yourself to the fear *as if it were* justified. Okay, so wait. You might be justifiably confused at this point. Are you supposed to avoid thinking about a situation or expose yourself to the situation? This is exactly the question to ask, and the answer is to do both, although it requires a mindful approach. Open up to the experience exactly as it is (mindfulness), lean into what that feels like (exposure), don't try to fix it (response prevention), then allow it to resolve by moving forward (the dialectic). There is that pesky skill again, mindfulness. It is a skill that helps in both ERP and DBT, and so we strongly encourage you to practice it.

Skillful Coping

In typical development, the older we get, the more skillful we become in all aspects of physical, emotional, cognitive, and psychological abilities. If this were not the case, none of us would ever be able to leave home. We aren't born with a software package of skills, and the more complex skills that we need to handle life's difficulties, such as emotion regulation skills, must be learned. And then, even if and when you've learned how to regulate your emotions, less-skillful behaviors can still show up when life feels overwhelming and stressful. Even emotionally healthy people have been known to punch a wall or drink too much when overwhelmed, or use the behavior of denial by ignoring the consequences of potentially dangerous acts like unprotected sex, fast driving, or excessive drug use. Punching a wall, drinking excessively, and denial are not skillful coping strategies, even if they are temporarily effective.

Skillful coping is the most effective way to disengage from repetitive behaviors and unproductive actions, rumination, and other mental rituals. For Gladys, arranging to have a friend pick her up for work, for instance, would be a skillful coping mechanism, because she would have to focus on a value system that prioritizes other people's time over her own personal belongings. In other words, she'll no longer be able to keep turning around to check her door, as doing so would make her feel guilty about keeping her friend waiting; not only that, but prioritizing her friend's time is a form of exposure to her fear!

Now, it is important that Gladys not compensate for the use of effective coping with a behavior that would allow the original compulsion to persist. For instance, waking up earlier than normal so she has enough time to repeatedly check the door would defeat the purpose of skillful coping. If she were to compensate in such a way to perpetuate the compulsive checking behavior, there could be other consequences to that, such as a detrimental impact to her sleep quality and energy level and the continued validation of her unjustified fear.

Compulsing Is a Wolf in Sheep's Clothing

We use the term "compulsing" to signify the persistent and repetitive performance of an action without it leading to a functional or clear reward. Compulsions are behaviors aimed at creating certainty when, much to our frustration, certainty is not truly attainable. It is possible that compulsing leads to the temporary disappearance of intrusive and unwanted thoughts and related unpleasant feelings, even the illusion of certainty, but this experience is temporary and ultimately sends the signal to your brain that compulsions are necessary and that your fears must be justified, thereby perpetuating the obsessive-compulsive cycle.

To the outside observer, though, compulsing might seem adaptive. It's relatively clear that it's maladaptive when a person with contamination OCD excessively washes their hands to control their fears about getting and then spreading germs. On the other hand, think of a surgeon with a handwashing compulsion. Here, handwashing is clearly appropriate as a preoperative procedure to ensure a sterile environment, and yet, at the same time, it is possible that the surgeon's excessive handwashing is a way to reduce OCD obsessions. The point is that certain extreme and repeated behaviors might not be compulsions, but simply observing someone doing that behavior does not tell you if it is compulsive or not. The surgeon should certainly continue the handwashing *and* address the OCD if it is causing distress outside of work.

Many people are familiar with the Albert Einstein quote: "Insanity is doing the same thing over and over again and expecting different results." Witty as this is and as applicable as it is to science experiments, we're not completely in agreement! In some cases, *sanity* is doing the same thing over and over again and expecting different results. Picture a child learning to ride a bike by practicing the same routine over and over until they can balance and not fall. The same applies to a cook who prepares the same meal repeatedly trying to get it right. So here's our revision to Einstein's doctrine: it makes sense to try the same thing repeatedly if you're in the process of learning; if, however, repeated attempts at the same thing keep you stuck in suffering, then you probably want to try something different.

Have a look at these examples of coping versus compulsing and determine whether your behaviors fall into either category.

Compulsing	Coping
Repeating behaviors over and over in order to experience certainty or until something is "just right" at the expense of other obligations	Accepting that you have done the best you can, that certainty would be ideal but you can tolerate some uncertainty in order to be able to meet your responsibilities
Filling every moment of downtime with a hyperfocused task to relieve the distress of not having gotten something just right	Filling your free moments building mastery in other areas of your life, such as learning to paint or to play a new sport or musical instrument
Avoiding other obligations or procrastinating tasks because of a fear that something else has not been done perfectly	Allowing yourself to notice the parts of your life that fulfill you, not only the parts that distress you

New Skill: Check the Facts

Before diving into the DBT skill of checking the facts, people with OCD and related disorders may be curious if "checking the facts" is different from compulsive ruminating or trying to figure out if your obsessions are "true" or not. Two suggestions may be helpful here. First, recognize that checking the facts is about separating what is known and observable from what is assumed and theorized. For example, you may know you're feeling tired right now and you can observe this from sensations in your body and a look in the mirror; but you may assume your fatigue means that you are getting sick and you may theorize that this illness will ruin your life. Well, as Ron Burgundy once said in *Anchorman*, "That escalated quickly!" Checking the facts isn't about separating true from false or trying to be certain you have the right answer. Second, consider how we described compulsions in the above table as repetitive, time-consuming, and at the expense of your obligations and values. So check the facts, yes, but pay attention to how much time you're spending checking the facts, how much willingness you have to accept the facts you observe, and how dependent you feel on this skill before you allow yourself to make a choice and move on.

Thoughts Are Not Facts

It can be difficult to recognize and then accept the idea that thoughts are not necessarily facts, especially when you are in a state of high emotions. But recognizing the difference between fact and opinion can keep you from behaving in self-destructive ways. If you think someone is going to attack you—simply because it is a thought, with no evidence of its truth—and you go punch that person, that could obviously lead to serious consequences.

How to Check the Facts

Step 1: Acknowledge that your brain generates a lot of thoughts. Say that to yourself: *My brain generates thoughts.*

Step 2: Recognize that not every thought is a truth, even if we believe it is. Some thoughts may be facts (*I got a D on my test*), but others are not necessarily so (*I am stupid*). One is an observation and the other is an assumption or value judgment.

Step 3: Determine that a statement is a fact rather than an opinion based on information that has concrete evidence—evidence that would be apparent to objective observers. If you say, "This is a brick that measures six inches across," other people would come to the same conclusion based on their observations. If you were to say, "This is a disgusting brick that belongs in a garbage dump," that is an opinion, and although others may conclude the same thing, they may not, because the statement is subjective (poor brick!).

Step 4: Label nonfactual thoughts as opinions or assumptions.

In sum, when you make certain kinds of statements, check whether each one is a fact or an opinion (remembering that facts, by definition, must contain actual and verifiable evidence).

Then there's the issue of whether or not the statement you believe is just a *preference*—a subjective determination of a specific choice between various options; for example: "Chocolate ice cream is way better than vanilla." The existence of ice cream is a fact; that it's gross is an opinion; but that you like one flavor over another is a preference. Here are some sample statements to consider:

- I have no friends.

- Nobody likes me.

- I don't deserve a promotion.

- I will fail this test.

- I like art classes over math.

- I am five feet tall.

- I am overweight.

- My eyes are blue.

- My eyes are ugly.

- I like people with brown eyes.

- I am single.

- I will be single forever.

- I am terrible at my job.

- Jon and Blaise are brilliant.

Now make a list of the kinds of statements *you* make and determine what category they fall into (following the example given):

statement	fact	opinion	preference
I am stupid.	✗	✓	✗

Another way to check the facts is to literally check with other people. If you think, *No one likes me*, ask twenty people if they like you. You may in fact turn out to be correct, but we've never met a single person for whom that is true. That said, it can certainly feel true and having that feeling is pretty awful.

Then What?

Mostly when people mistake thoughts for facts, that leads to the generation of strong emotions. Go back to one of the statements you made about yourself in the above table—a self-critical statement. Then consider:

1. What is the emotion you experience when you think that thought?

2. Do you want to change that emotion?

3. What event or interaction prompted the emotion?

4. Describe the facts you observed through your senses that led you to that thought (remembering that facts require objective evidence). Use your senses: What did you see, smell, taste, hear, or touch?

5. Label judgments as judgments and notice all-or-nothing and black-and-white descriptions.

6. What are your interpretations, assumptions, and conclusion of what happened?

7. Are there other possible interpretations of the event?

8. Test your interpretations and assumptions to see if they fit the facts based on objective evidence.

9. Does your emotional reaction fit the facts of the situation, or does it fit your assumptions and interpretations of the situation?

10. Finally, if the behaviors or actions you are considering pursuing in response to your thought/emotion are consistent with the actual, evidential facts, are these behaviors or actions consistent with your long-term goals?

PRACTICE: What are some unhelpful ways you use compulsing?

_____

_____

_____

_____

What are some ways you use skillful coping?

_____

_____

_____

Of your more helpful coping skills, which do you find particularly nourishing or adding of value to your experience?

_____

_____

What unwanted compulsing experiences would it benefit you to stand up to and resist?

_____

_____

_____

What unwanted thoughts and feelings tend to lead you to ineffective, maladaptive, or unwise behaviors and are better turned away from?

_____

_____

_____

CHAPTER 7

Engaging Your Thoughts and Emotions Skillfully vs. Escalating Your Distress

Zachary is a thirty-four-year-old businessman who works in an office building down the street from the local elementary school. Every day, he drives past the school in the morning as the kids are arriving off the bus. A few weeks ago, he was watching his favorite police drama on TV and a character on the show was arrested for sexually abusing a child. The next morning on his usual route to work, he saw the children arriving at school and had a thought about the character in the show. Immediately, he felt anxious and disgusted at himself for thinking of a pedophile while children were in his view. What if this meant something about him? What if he snapped and did something to a child?

He started taking a much longer and less convenient route to work to avoid seeing the children in the hopes of avoiding unwanted thoughts. He also stopped watching his favorite TV show because it triggered the thoughts. He started spending hours online researching the difference between a normal intrusive thought and a sign that you could be a danger to children. Thankfully, his compulsive research led him to a website that explained that his worries could be due to OCD and could be treated.

He started seeing a therapist, who assigned him some exposure and response prevention exercises, such as making sure to drive by the school and stopping avoidance of his unwanted triggering thoughts. Though some of the exposures were more tolerable than others, he often found himself driven to tears and panic whenever he still had unwanted thoughts. Instead of reassuring himself, he would purposely make the thoughts bigger and more upsetting to prove that he didn't like the thoughts, and he would repeatedly tell himself he's probably a pedophile. He gets so upset at times that he starts to hyperventilate and hit himself.

Zachary is clearly having a difficult go of it. Although he was greatly relieved to have a diagnostic name to attach to his woes (OCD), the taboo thoughts of harming children and the consequent catastrophic thoughts of his life being ruined because of them are causing a lot of distress. His therapist has wisely instructed him to not avoid his triggers (recall that avoidance only teaches the brain that triggers are dangerous), but Zachary needs to be able to experience his triggers without getting so overwhelmed that he loses sight of the goal of his treatment.

When he exposes himself to his fears, he of course feels uncomfortable. But if he sticks with exposure, he will eventually learn that his unwanted thoughts are junk mail that doesn't need any special attention. However, when he is still in the uncomfortable phase of exposure, if he begins to engage in mental rituals, self-criticism, or other behaviors that make his distress rise too high, he won't be able to remain present enough to actually learn that he can tolerate the discomfort. What a trap of thoughts and feelings!

We want Zachary to skillfully engage his thoughts and emotions (by doing exposure to what scares him), but we do not want him to escalate his distress to the level that he becomes more focused on self-hatred or self-harm than on overcoming his OCD.

Engaging Thoughts and Emotions with ERP

In regard to Zachary's thoughts, he would benefit from turning his avoidant behavior around and doing the things that reliably bring on his unwanted thoughts—that is, driving the usual route to work and watching his TV show, even though he knows they may be triggering. He might even benefit from doing some imaginal exposures, like writing out a story in which he describes snapping and turning into someone that harms a child. It could also be useful for him to recognize his cognitive distortions, such as catastrophizing and magnifying the significance of his unwanted thoughts.

Take a moment to consider the types of unwanted thoughts that trigger you into avoidance. Notice how even just thinking of these triggers changes the way you feel in the body. While engaging these thoughts, you, like Zachary, will experience some anxiety and will want to reteach your brain that you do not need compulsions in response to that anxiety. In addition to eliminating the compulsion of avoidance, it is also beneficial to resist efforts to analyze or make sense of the thoughts—that is the "response prevention" of ERP. Consider the ways you may use mental behavior to compulsively analyze or reassure yourself away from your unwanted thoughts.

Zachary's OCD has conditioned him to avoid and analyze to keep himself and others safe, so changing that conditioning is going to be met with some resistance in the mind. Similarly, your behavior has conditioned your brain to avoid the things that feel unsafe, and naturally, you would expect your brain to resist changing this. That's a good thing! If it were too easy to convince our brains that something is safe, we would make some foolish decisions. By engaging with the unwanted thoughts and demonstrating to the brain that you can handle their presence without avoidance and analysis, you can gradually turn the fear learning into safety learning.

Though it's courageous and wise to challenge yourself to get better, it's important to engage with your unwanted thoughts and emotions *skillfully* to bring on a level of intensity that you can handle without losing sight of your goals. What skills are we talking about specifically?

- In vivo exposure to being near triggers

- Imaginal exposures to confront fears

- Recognizing and abandoning rumination and other mental rituals

- Recognizing and abandoning cognitive distortions

How can you engage skillfully with your unwanted thoughts and emotions using ERP principles?

_____

_____

_____

_____

Escalating Your Distress to the Point of Losing the Plot

Zachary made a few strategic mistakes in his zeal to overcome his obsession. First and foremost, he used his exposure as a form of *testing* and tried to make himself as fearful as possible to prove he hated his unwanted thoughts. While turning up the heat can be useful, nobody likes burnt toast. Working yourself to the point of total overwhelm interferes with being able to see the thoughts clearly and navigate the distress they are already conditioned to come with.

Another tactical error Zachary made here is telling himself he's "probably" a pedophile. This might seem like a good exposure idea at first, but adding "probably" to the question invites judgment and analysis. The end result is that he just feels disgusted with himself rather than capable of accepting uncertainty. Accepting uncertainty doesn't mean assuming the worst. It just means letting go of analysis and of trying to be certain about the odds.

Finally, in times of overwhelming distress, Zachary hits himself, which is not only maladaptive and potentially dangerous, but adds nothing useful to the treatment. ERP can certainly be scary, but ultimately, such behaviors make ERP ineffective and simply torturous.

What are some things you think, do, or tell yourself when doing exposures to your unwanted thoughts that actually make them so intolerable that you can't really learn from them?

_____

_____

_____

_____

When the Distress Is Too Intense

When your distress escalates to the point that you are completely overwhelmed and not able to pay attention mindfully to your exposures, DBT's distress tolerance and emotion regulation skills can be used to down-regulate without turning to total avoidance or other compulsions.

If you get to a point in ERP where you feel completely out of control, you can pull yourself back with a mindful awareness exercise. Sure signs that things have escalated beyond their usefulness are intense feelings of self-loathing, depersonalization, or dissociation (a feeling like you are no longer present or in your body) and urges to hurt yourself or others. In this case, mindfulness of body sensations in the context of thoughts can be helpful. The following exercise is a way to register what is happening in your body without giving in to unhelpful or harmful behaviors.

Practice: Body Awareness

This exercise is divided into three parts of five minutes each, for a total of fifteen minutes. You'll focus on your lower body, your upper body, then your head. To start, sit comfortably in a chair with your feet on the floor. Ideally, choose a quiet place where you are not likely to be interrupted. You can do this exercise with your eyes open or closed, but if you get distracted with your eyes open, then close them; if you doze off with your eyes closed, then open them. Setting your phone's timer for five-minute intervals will keep you in the exercise instead of watching the clock.

Part 1: Awareness of Your Lower Body (5 minutes)

Sit in your chair and notice the feel of your feet on the ground. (Tip: Wearing socks or going barefoot will provide better feedback than wearing shoes.) Start with attention on your toes, then your soles, up through your ankles. Move awareness to your calves, your knees, then your thighs. Feel the sensation of your thighs and then your buttocks against the chair. Notice how each part of your lower body feels. Are your feet tired or sore? Do they elicit any thoughts? As you go from one part of the lower body to the next, breathe in slowly and breathe out slowly.

Part 2: Awareness of Your Upper Body (5 minutes)

Place your hands on your stomach. Notice the sensations, inside and out. Can you feel gurgling? Do you feel hungry? Do you have butterflies in your stomach as you notice anxiety? Move your attention to the lower back. Notice the sensations as it rests against the back of the chair. Do you notice tension or backache? As you move from one part of your upper body to the next, breathe in slowly and out slowly. If you notice hunger or back tension, just notice—you don't have to do anything with these sensations right now. If your mind gets distracted, gently return to noticing.

Next, move your awareness to your chest and upper back; again, as you move from one part of your upper body to another, breathe in slowly and out slowly. Keep noticing sensations and thoughts. You might become aware of your breathing, and you can label it as shallow or deep. You might notice your heartbeat—it might be pounding, or it could be fast or slow. Label any thoughts and sensations as they arise.

Now bring your awareness to your arms. Move your hands from your stomach to rest on your lap. Starting with your fingertips, scan your fingers, the back of your hands, your palms. Are your hands open or clenched? Continue this practice as you move up through the forearms, elbows, biceps, triceps, and shoulders. Take a slow breath in and out at each body part as you notice.

Part 3: Awareness of Your Head (5 minutes)

Shift your focus from your shoulders to your neck. These areas often tense up with stress. Do you notice tension in the muscles? Are your shoulders and neck relaxed? Take a slow breath in and a slow breath out. Breath is emphasized in exercises like these because slowing the breath slows the mind for a lot of people with distress.

Now move to your head. Notice your jaw, your chin, your mouth, your nose, eyes, and ears. Do you notice any physical sensations or tension (especially in the jaw area)? Notice how your whole head feels. Do you have a headache? Some people have such persistent low-grade headaches, they hardly notice them. Now notice your thoughts. Has your mind started to wander or worry? If it has, gently bring your attention back to your body scan.

As a final optional step, keep a diary of your body awareness practice to allow for better insights into how you physically feel as a result of your use of DBT and ERP. For instance, you might notice tension in some parts of your body that you hadn't noticed before. Or you might find that doing regular exercise or relaxation techniques reduces your overall level of stress and worry.

Engaging your thoughts and emotions means challenging yourself to confront what scares you in a way that is productive and educational. Escalating your distress means going out of your way to make your thoughts and emotions so intolerable that all you can focus on is escaping them. Overcoming them effectively requires being able to stay in their presence and respond differently, so revving things up past the point of tolerability doesn't allow you to get the work done.

Can you identify the difference in your own struggles between engaging and escalating?

_____

_____

_____

When can you use mindfulness skills to walk yourself back from overwhelm while engaging in ERP?

_____

_____

CHAPTER 8

Accepting Unwanted Thoughts vs. Believing Untruths

Twenty-nine-year-old Mark is an aspiring author whose most recent manuscript was returned, unread, with a generic note telling him that the publishing house doesn't take unsolicited manuscripts. The self-critical thoughts start right up: I'm so stupid for believing that anyone would want to read my work. I'm not meant to be an author. He then wonders if he should have used the Oxford comma, and this worry begins to plague him and becomes intrusive. He's been diagnosed with OCD and is thus aware of the danger of starting to obsess about the Oxford comma. Now he wants to go through his entire book again to analyze his punctuation.

Untrue Beliefs

These days, it's hard to know what or whom to believe. In politics, the term "fake news" is used to refer to information that is completely untrue, contains only partial truths, or is demonstrably false. The term can also be applied to the way the brain works. The problem is that "fake news" is often very believable—in terms of this book, it's less about external sources of fake news, untruths, and unwanted thoughts and more about the sources generated by your own brain.

Before we expand further on this, a little historical digression. In May 1897, the author Mark Twain was on a speaking tour in London when news reached the US that he'd grown very ill and had died. Two quotes are attributed to him in response: "The reports of my death are greatly exaggerated" and "The rumors of my death have been greatly exaggerated." Neither of these actually came from Twain. In a letter to a journalist, Twain instead wrote: "I can understand perfectly how the report of my illness got about, I have even heard on good authority that I was dead. [My cousin] was ill in London two or three weeks ago, but is well now. The report of my illness grew out of this illness. The report of my death was an exaggeration."

It takes a bit of research to get to what actually happened, and, really, there was little reason to question the news at the time, particularly when it seemed so plausible and the quotes seemed so Twain-like. And yet this is what happens all the time: we hear some external news story or listen to some internal thought and immediately take it as truth.

This example of distortion has to do with wording; however, we see the impact of untrue beliefs in everyday life, with some significant consequences. You might remember the 2016 case of Edgar Maddison Welch, who believed a story he heard on a conspiracy theory radio show about a prominent politician abusing children in the basement of a Washington, DC, pizza shop. Despite his friends and others telling him it wasn't true, he believed the false story. So he armed himself with weapons and showed up at the pizza joint only to find that no children were being abused; in fact, the restaurant didn't even have a basement. But the false belief had been planted, he'd believed it and acted upon it, and it could have had tragic consequences beyond Welch's arrest and imprisonment.

Returning to Mark, he's stuck in obsessive thinking—repeated, persistent, and unwanted thoughts that are intrusive and cause distress or anxiety. Mark is not only being hypercritical and judgmental, believing the untrue story that his manuscript was not reviewed because of his lack of use of the Oxford comma, but he is at risk of having his unwanted thoughts solidly planted in his mind, where they can grow to the point of becoming debilitating.

Yes, Mark received some unwanted news—the publishing house doesn't accept unsolicited manuscripts—but his mind took this information and turned it into a criticism of himself, and now he's having intrusive thoughts about his work being unworthy solely on the basis of commas.

Interestingly, evidence shows that most of us experience intrusive thoughts. Even people who don't have anxiety or other mental health conditions have such thoughts as swerving their car into oncoming traffic, hurting a loved one, developing a terminal illness, heeding impulses to do something shameful, or saying obscene things out loud in public.

The difference between intrusive thoughts in someone with anxiety versus someone without anxiety is the way in which the thoughts are appraised. If you have a condition such as OCD or clinical anxiety, you are more likely to judge the intrusive thoughts as bad, immoral, or destructive. When you judge or interpret the thoughts this way, this typically leads to an emotional response that tells you, *Hey, that's an important thought.* Then, when your brain does this, it further focuses your brain on the thought, and it all becomes a vicious cycle.

If you have OCD or a related condition, you are more likely to spend more time thinking about the consequences and implications of these thoughts and then take measures to prevent some dreaded outcome from occurring. You may feel a sense of moral urgency to address the thoughts. What happens to people who don't have clinical anxiety? They tend to dismiss these thoughts as odd, let them go, then carry on with what they were doing.

So, if we understood the futility of dwelling in untrue beliefs and learned to accept unwanted thoughts, wouldn't life be so much easier? How do we do this? The way to start is to distinguish between an unwanted thought and a false belief (though of course there is sometimes an overlap). But let's start with Mark's case. He thinks, *I'm so stupid for believing that anyone would want to read my work; I'm not meant to be an author.* Having this thought play over and over in his brain would make it an unwanted thought, but is it true or untrue?

To answer that, let's look at Mark's thought processes in detail. First, he's basing his "stupidity" on the fact that the publisher did not accept his unsolicited manuscript. Second, he's concluding that no one would ever want to read his material just because this publisher didn't. Third, Mark believes that all this means he is not meant to be an author. Of course it was disappointing to have his manuscript returned unread, but the thoughts Mark has in response to that are simply not true. In fact, the only conclusion based on the facts is that the publishing house does not take unsolicited manuscripts. Mark's thought is an untrue belief.

Here are common statements we hear:

- "I can't tell somebody the truth because they will judge me."

- "If I get close to people, I destroy the relationship and always get hurt."

- "People are all untrustworthy, and because of that, they will all betray me."

- "I can't go after something I want because I don't know what I'd do if I got rejected, or if I got accepted and then failed."

- "If someone doesn't give me a birthday card, it means they don't care."

What are your untrue beliefs? Write down a few here: _____

_____

_____

Now, all of these statements are based on some previous experience—we're not saying they came out of nowhere. But when you have these types of thoughts, it is often the case that you have taken a past experience and concluded that all future experiences will have the same outcome. So, yes, untrue beliefs tend to have their roots in some past experience, and there also tends to be some evidence to support your conclusion. However, when you engage in the cognitive distortion known as *overgeneralization* (introduced in chapter 3), you reach a conclusion about *one* past event and then incorrectly apply it to *all* similar events.

Mark overgeneralized about his returned manuscript. Can you think of some situations in which you overgeneralize?

Here is where we want you to use the skill of mindful assessment to observe the thought, describe the thought, then determine if it represents the truth. To practice this, you can use notecards or a notes app to record some of your automatic thoughts en route to determining when you're engaging in overgeneralization. By catching automatic, typically negative thoughts, you're able to recognize that they're based on very little, if any, evidence and thus label the thoughts as untrue.

However, let's say you *do* have evidence that something is factually true. For instance, if Mark has repeatedly been told that his writing is not good, that he needs to do a lot more work on it, and that he should take writing classes, then he does have some evidence that his belief about himself is accurate. But this doesn't mean he has no talent and no chance of being an author. If you've had repeated failures in relationships, then you may indeed need some help figuring this out, but coming to the conclusion that you are terrible at all relationships after one failed date would be an untrue belief.

Unwanted Thoughts

Mark is worried that his current experience is going to lead him back to the struggles he's had with his OCD. He's noticing the repeated thought that his manuscript was rejected because he didn't use a specific type of comma and the urge to go back into his writing and check all the commas. Now the thought is playing over and over: *It's not perfect; my commas need to be perfect if I'm going to succeed as a writer.*

Unwanted thoughts like these are not useful and plague us. Yet however much we try, knowing the thoughts are useless doesn't end them, does it? They enter the mind, stay there, and repeat over and over. Some people are so deeply tormented by them, they become unable to assess things without distortion.

One way to work with these thoughts is to pay attention to the events and conclusions that led to them. For Mark, it is the perceived rejection of his creative output. So his task is to let himself drop below the thoughts, recognize the emotions associated with his perceived rejection, accept the situation as it accurately is rather than as he has concluded it is, and then allow himself to feel the emotions that led to the unwanted thoughts so they can decrease in intensity. More specifically, we want him to notice that using the skill of willingness to feel the emotions that led to his unwanted thoughts will calm the emotions and that in turn will make the thoughts less loud. In other words, accepting unwanted thoughts in the context of their underlying emotions leads to a lessening of their impact.

Before proceeding with how to deal with unwanted thoughts, another brief digression. Aristotle is attributed as saying that "nature abhors a vacuum;" this means that unfilled spaces go against the laws of nature and physics and that every space needs to be filled with something. In a similar vein, the brain doesn't seem to like not having thoughts. Take a minute to observe all that is going on in your brain right now. It's likely your mind is swimming in thoughts, some connected to what you're doing right now and others that seem totally unrelated. The nature of the mind is for it to be filled with thoughts, and if some of your thoughts are unwanted, repetitive, and causing you distress, recognize what happens if you just focus on those thoughts versus if you skillfully attend to some other focus.

Shifting your focus in this way is a changed behavior. And when people change behaviors, their thoughts also change. So adding the cognitive element—targeting your thoughts directly—is a powerful tool for change.

What does this look like in reality instead of just theory? Well, returning to Mark, he first needs to see that his state of distress is originating from his thought that his lack of use of the Oxford comma has made his writing unacceptable. He then needs to recognize and accept that this thought is irrational, to challenge himself not to believe it, and to replace it with a more accurate or helpful thought like, *Not everyone uses the Oxford comma, and if it is in fact important, an editor will catch it.*

The skill of mindfulness helps identify the patterns of thought that lead to our suffering. Without mindful awareness, thoughts take on a life of their own and have us concluding things that just aren't so. Mindful compassion is recognizing our unwanted thoughts, accepting that we have them, and then, without judgment, being willing to challenge them. Unwanted thoughts include feelings of unworthiness, failure, sadness, attachment, and clinging. Self-compassion is to mindfully transforming your thoughts as an act of self-validation and self-healing.

Now, this is not going to happen overnight. Retraining your mind requires steady, patient, and repeated effort. You don't train to run a marathon by jogging once around the block, but instead you begin to run regularly, slowly transforming your leg muscles just like the power of *neuroplasticity* (the ability of the brain to form and reorganize the connections between brain cells in response to new learning or experience) slowly but steadily trains or retrains the brain to think things differently. Not every thought, just like every run, is going to feel as good as others, so sometimes challenging your thoughts can feel very mechanical. This doesn't matter. What's important is that you engage with more beneficial thoughts gently, over and over again, to relieve your suffering.

Uncertainty and Untruthiness

If your brains can make up words, so can ours! A key factor in navigating unwanted thoughts is accepting uncertainty. If you have social anxiety, accepting uncertainty that others may evaluate you negatively can feel overwhelming. If you have borderline personality disorder, accepting uncertainty that someone will reject you can seem near impossible. So cognitive behavioral treatments typically emphasize uncertainty acceptance, even when they employ cognitive interventions that may help you weigh in objectively on how much things are really worth worrying about.

Any sentence that starts with "maybe" is objectively true. True, but not necessarily likely or worth attention. Maybe it will rain today. That is an objectively true statement. Maybe the sun will explode today? Still objectively true, but it's an extraordinary claim that defies everything we know about physics, so probably best to ignore it. In ERP, we are actively trying to engage with the things that scare us, that bring us uncertainty (what we don't know) and doubt (what we know but lack confidence in).

But this doesn't mean we need to buy into things that are clearly not based in any kind of reasonable assumption of truth.

For example, an intrusive thought about having hit someone with your car might come with urges to drive back to check, even when there is no evidence that you hit anything. Choosing not to go back means accepting uncertainty that maybe somehow, in some way, you hit someone without knowing it and the absence of evidence is just some kind of bizarre illusion. Yes, *maybe* you hit something (just like maybe the sun will blow up today), but allowing for that possibility doesn't make it the truth. And spending the rest of the day calling yourself a murderer is not necessarily the best intervention, even if it seems like exposure. A better strategy would be to let go of resistance to the fact that you cannot have certainty about your fear and move forward in your life as if you are not a murderer. You don't do this by repeatedly reassuring yourself of your innocence (that would be as compulsive as checking), but by actually moving forward and reengaging with the present while making space for uncomfortable feelings. Accepting uncertainty does not mean assuming you are bad..

Now it's your turn:

What are some situations in which you can work on accepting an unwanted thought?

_____

_____

_____

_____

_____

What are some useful learning ideas or replacement thoughts or action items you can substitute for the unwanted thoughts?

_____

_____

_____

_____

_____

What are four untruths (thoughts for which there is no factual evidence) you believe?

_____

_____

_____

_____

List some facts that challenge these untruths:

_____

_____

_____

_____

_____

_____

CHAPTER 9

Distracting from Unwise Behaviors vs. Avoiding the Hard Things

Desiree really wants to overcome her fear of blood-borne illnesses. Since she started avoiding anything that might have even a molecule of blood on it, she's found herself avoiding nearly everything. If she has to touch something triggering, like a trash bin (someone could have thrown a bandage away in that!), she white-knuckles her way through it and tries to distract herself by remembering the lyrics to her favorite songs. She then carefully tracks everything she might have touched on her way to go take a shower so she can go back and decontaminate or avoid anything in her house that triggers her.

In her efforts to utilize ERP, she found that even something that sounds like it should be easy quickly overwhelms her. She then gets angry at herself for being weak. This sometimes escalates into calling herself stupid and worthless, and rather than invest in her exposures, she sometimes ends up simply pacing around her house, calling herself names and focusing on how she wishes she was never born, until she finally collapses in tears.

You Don't Have to Dwell on Your Unwanted Thoughts

In the world of treating unwanted thoughts, we used to believe that *thought-stopping*, or literally trying to block ourselves from experiencing thoughts, would work. Strategies range from snapping a rubber band every time an unwanted thought arises to literally thinking of a stop sign when the thought shows up. What we now understand is that putting too much effort into avoiding unwanted thoughts simply makes them louder. Try not thinking of a pink elephant right now and you get the idea. Even more interesting, it turns out brains aren't particularly good at subtracting or deleting thoughts, just adding to them. So thought-stopping efforts tend to just make unwanted thoughts the very things we add thought-stopping effort to! If you struggle with unwanted thoughts, you've probably had well-meaning friends, even therapists, tell you to just stop thinking about them, but that is easier said than done.

Still, even with an evolved understanding of how to respond to thoughts, we sometimes overcorrect and confuse the absence of thought-stopping with an emphasis on dwelling on our unwanted thoughts. Paying mindful attention to thoughts and feelings in exposure certainly can be skillful, but paying too much attention to thoughts and feelings that have spun out of control can also be a problem, especially if you are prone to emotion dysregulation.

The distinction to make here is between being aware of what you are thinking and being "lost in thought." To be lost in thought is to fully identify with the stories in your head, failing to recognize that they are stories. When you dream, everything seems to make sense, even if you're flying on a mountain goat through a mall that closed down years ago. When you wake up and realize you were dreaming, it seems odd how real it felt. Most of the time, when we're awake at least, we can catch ourselves getting consumed by our thoughts, getting carried away in both negative and positive daydreams. Some people are more susceptible to getting absorbed into their stories and may have to turn their attention away from thoughts with intention. If your mind is telling you to hurt yourself and your body is telling you that it's completely out of control, then focusing closely on those thoughts and urges may be unwise. You might get sucked into the dream-like story and lose yourself in the plot. In those situations, it's better to distract yourself for a bit and check in with yourself later when things have calmed down.

Skillful Distraction

Distraction can also play a strategic role in exposure therapy when it is used specifically to broaden your attention. For example, if you are exposing yourself to contamination and are vigilantly focusing on where your hand is and what it's touching, trying to think of your favorite movie may rob you of the full exposure experience. However, ruminating over what you touched and what you're going to touch next is *also* taking you out of the experience.

To effectively confront your unwanted thoughts with exposure, you want to be engaged with the entirety of the present experience as it is. Fantasizing about not being in the exposure while simultaneously trying to do the exposure falls flat. You can open up to paying attention to other things happening in the room because you are still there with the experience. You can even have a conversation with someone so long as you're willing to do it while maintaining some awareness of the thoughts and feelings of contamination.

Lastly, distraction can help disengage from rumination and other mental rituals. If you are ruminating, you may find yourself trying to figure out whether or not the exposure is safe or trying to determine if your thoughts are acceptable. You might be repeatedly reassuring yourself about the thought, engaging in mental chanting or counting, or analyzing the thought in some other way. In other words, trying to get certain in your head can be just as compulsive as washing your hands. So watching your favorite movie and *really* paying attention to it is going to interfere with remembering the order in which you touched contaminated objects. In fact, allowing yourself to be distracted can actually be the exposure! This is especially the case when you are focused on being vigilant as a safety strategy.

Ego-Syntonic and Ego-Dystonic Thoughts Revisited

Another important distinction to be made here when discussing distraction as opposed to avoidance is the difference between ego-dystonic and ego-syntonic thoughts. As explained in chapter 1, ego-dystonic thoughts are not in line with our assumed identity, it doesn't make sense to us why we are having them, and we find them intrusive and incongruent with what seems reasonable to think. In a sense, recognizing that you are having intrusive ego-dystonic thoughts suggests there is a rational mind observing what is going on and reacting with alarm.

On the contrary, ego-syntonic thoughts feel in line with who we are, make sense to us, even seem like wisdom, including when they are very dark and could potentially lead to unhealthy or harmful behaviors. Ego-syntonic thoughts can be perceived as unwanted (they make you unhappy and you wish they weren't there) without being intrusive (you expect them to be there given how you feel in the moment). If you are having self-hating thoughts or thoughts about hurting yourself (or others) that seem like they make a fair amount of sense, then it suggests that the lens you are using to distinguish helpful from unhelpful thoughts may be compromised. Looking through a clear lens, we can usually see things the way they actually are, but when the mind gets cluttered with unwanted thoughts and intense emotions, it can cloud our ability to be objective. In other words, best not to keep focusing on harmful ego-syntonic thoughts because they could lead you into unwise behaviors without you even realizing it. Catching and challenging cognitive distortions to help respond to thoughts rationally and using mindfulness skills to reduce emotional overwhelm are a bit like cleaning your mental lens.

So, we don't want to distract away to escape from ego-dystonic thoughts when we know rationally that exposure to them will make them more tolerable and less threatening. This is fundamental to exposure-based treatments (though mixing up attention and changing focus may also be useful in some exposures). But we also don't want to stay fused with ego-syntonic thoughts that can lead us to treating ourselves and others badly or in a manner inconsistent with our values. Here's a chart to help identify the difference between helpful and unhelpful distraction:

Unhelpful Distraction	Helpful Distraction
Trying not to feel unwanted feelings or have unwanted thoughts while intentionally doing exposure to a fear	Putting your mind on other subjects when your ego-syntonic self-hating or self-harming thoughts are too loud for you to think clearly
Filling every moment of downtime with a mindless task to avoid being present with thoughts and feelings	Giving your mind something else to do when you are trying to resist mental rituals
Avoiding or procrastinating tasks out of fear of not completing them perfectly	Allowing yourself to notice different areas of attention while distressed instead of only what distresses you
Engaging in distractions that offer no value beyond numbing yourself out	Engaging in distractions that add meaningfully to your experience and are in line with your values

Take a moment to consider an unwanted thought that tends to cause you distress.

What are some unhelpful ways you distract from this thought?

_____

_____

_____

_____

What are some skillful ways you distract from this thought?

_____

_____

_____

_____

How did you determine the difference between your unhelpful and skillful distraction?

_____

_____

_____

_____

Of your more helpful distractions, which do you find particularly nourishing or adding of value to your experience?

_____

_____

Which unwanted thoughts and feelings would it be beneficial for you to stand up to and resist distracting away from?

_____

_____

_____

Which unwanted thoughts and feelings tend to lead you to unhelpful or unwise behaviors and are better turned away from?

_____

_____

_____

_____

CHAPTER 10

Addressing Shame vs. Being Hijacked by Shame

Stephanie, thirty years old, has decided it's time to start dating after a ten-year hiatus. In college, men only wanted one-night stands when she wanted a relationship, and she was disappointed and hurt by how men treated her. Her friends at work have encouraged her to use a dating app, and despite her initial skepticism, she decides to give it a go. She knows some of her friends have had bad experiences on apps, and yet many have told her they still had fun on dates, even when they didn't evolve into relationships.

Her biggest concern is that she doesn't feel men are trustworthy. She trusted some in her past who had not been kind to her. One of her uncles had been sexually inappropriate with her, and although she did not feel abused by him, he'd made her feel uncomfortable in many ways after she'd started developing curves, like commenting on her body, hugging her too closely, running his fingers through her hair, and telling her she'd make some man very happy. Disgusted by his behavior, she told her parents, but they said she was making a big deal out of nothing. She started to have negative thoughts about herself, including the belief that she must have given her uncle "subconscious hints" to invite his behavior and that she must be a "slut." The one person she could turn to, a beloved maternal aunt, had died when Stephanie was fifteen.

Dating had always been difficult for her. Ever since puberty, she'd been ashamed of her body and had started wearing baggy sweaters to cover her physique. She didn't care how hot they made her in summer; she just didn't want anyone commenting on her body. When all her friends had started dating, she'd desperately wanted to date as well, but she refused to take off the baggy clothes and care for her hair. If she looked good, her thinking went, then men would use flattery to try to manipulate her into a sexual relationship like her uncle had. Men simply couldn't be trusted, she told herself over and over.

After college, just when she was considering dating again, that abruptly came to a halt when she saw her uncle again at a family Thanksgiving gathering. When he complimented her looks and smiled at her creepily, the childhood memories came flooding back and, along with them, a torrent of negative self-thoughts.

Nevertheless, Stephanie is now pushing herself to try online dating. It's an important first step, but she still continues to hide her body under baggy clothes and neglect her self-care. If someone is going to like her, she wants it to be because of her and not her appearance.

The Nature of Shame

Shame is a painful emotion—the experience of feeling like you are not good enough, that you are unworthy or inadequate. How does such an awful feeling evolve? From a DBT perspective, all emotions have useful functions. They can also have unhelpful consequences. From an evolutionary point of view, the function of shame was to get us to change or hide behavior that threatened to get us kicked out of our community. Imagine the early cave dweller who was not carrying his weight in terms of the needs of the group. If his actions led to the extreme disapproval of his clan because they were not consistent with the expectations of its members, then being rejected by the group would have meant having to survive on his own, and thousands of years ago, that would have been a very difficult thing to do. In this way, the function of the emotion of shame would have been to encourage him to act in a way that kept him with his people.

But we are not cave people any longer, so here is a contemporary example of when shame functions as it should. A man is not paying child support to his ex-wife and instead uses the money to gamble. His child is struggling at school because she doesn't have enough food and warm clothes. Our community would deem this behavior objectionable, and when found out, he would feel shame.

This is an example of *justified* shame—justified because it fits the facts. Put another way, shame is justified when there is a real danger of getting rejected by one's social group. Our society would typically reject this father for failing to meet his obligations, at great cost to his child. When shame is justified, it doesn't mean you should hate yourself. On the contrary, it means your moral integrity alarm system is working well. Justified shame is like a buffer zone for keeping you safely within society's moral framework, so shame can be an important reminder to change course and choose wiser behaviors. However, much like the overreactive fear response in anxiety disorders, an overreactive shame response can make you feel bad even when you're well within the safety zone.

Stephanie's shame is *unjustified* because it doesn't fit the facts. She has done nothing wrong, and there is little risk of being rejected by society for dating someone, for having a human body, for just being who she is. Also, even though her uncle has caused her distress, nothing she's done has violated anything she believes in. (Her obsessive mind may be telling her she cannot trust that this is true, but *thoughts* are not proof of *actions*!)

Nevertheless, like many people who have experienced what Stephanie has, she feels her shame is justified. She feels she has done something wrong, even though she'd never feel that way about someone else who's experienced what she has. Logically, she can see the fallacy in her thinking, but her sense of shame is powerful, in large part because she blames herself for what happened. When this type of powerful yet unjustified shame takes over, it can make people feel flawed, unlovable, and worthless. Given how she feels about herself, Stephanie is at risk for getting into abusive relationships.

Is Shame the Same as Guilt?

We digress for a moment to address this important issue of confusing shame and guilt. One quick way to distinguish between the two is to consider the type of statement that arises with each. Guilt shows up when you've done something wrong or crossed your values, and it tends to be a specific behavior: "I did wrong." Shame is the experience of a more global assessment of the self: "I am bad."

Think about times in your life when you've felt each of these emotions and list a few here.

Shame: _____

_____

_____

Guilt: _____

_____

_____

So What Should We Do About Shame?

Let's start with justified shame. If you've done something that crossed the values and standards of your community, the best remedy is to correct it. Let's be clear—we're talking about actual external evidence that you made a poor choice that had a negative impact on someone or is inconsistent with your values. We're not talking about a "what if" thought or a negative mental assumption about the quality of your actions. In the above example, the man should take ownership of his responsibilities and pay his child support.

To some extent, shame lies behind the theory of punishment for misdeeds, such as imprisonment. As the saying goes: "You do the crime, you do the time." Once we have recognized our transgression and atoned for it, our society lets us back in (at least, we hope so). In truth, some people struggle to reenter a family or society with a clean slate after atoning; similarly, you may struggle to let yourself start over even after you've atoned for your transgression, or the people around you may still judge you. When shame hangs around, it can be difficult to dislodge.

Healthy or justified shame can be looked at as a protective buffer that allows us to be skeptical of our moral obsessions. It keeps us from being so convinced of our awesomeness that we cause others pain without realizing or caring (consider how many times you've referred to your least-favorite politician as "having no shame"). Justified shame can be viewed as a warning sign, an almost friendly reminder to back up and take a look at how we're behaving and ask if it fits our values and those embraced by our community.

But for unjustified shame, as there has been no transgression (even if you think there has been), the best approach to tackle it is repeated exposure to the triggers that prompt it. For Stephanie, this means wearing clothes that don't hide her curves. This is the skill of opposite action put into action! We choose opposite action because we want to show the brain that the shame is the opposite of justified. And although it's easy to advise using this skill, it can be very aversive. Truthfully, almost all forms of exposure therapy are aversive, so hold in mind the things that will motivate you to keep going. In Stephanie's case, the motivation to try a dating app is to have an enduring romantic relationship. However, she also recognizes that there are consequences to not tending to her appearance. This is an avoidance behavior that protects her from the painful emotions elicited by her uncle's actions, and it's a behavior that has prevented her from achieving her goal.

Her task meets at the intersection of DBT and ERP, which would prescribe her to:

1. Self-validate that what happened to her was very painful

2. Radically accept that her experiences were in her past

3. Expose herself to noticing her curves and her hair and all the thoughts associated with this exposure

4. Block the two prominent maladaptive behaviors of wearing baggy clothes and not doing her hair (over time, maybe also identify other behaviors that serve the function of avoidance)

5. Block or prevent inaccurate representations of herself or escape behaviors, such as being vague, blaming herself or others, or avoiding the exposure

6. Remind herself of her goal to resume dating

7. Repeat this process over and over again

Remember, in ERP terms, Stephanie is changing her conditioned pairing. Curves = slut? No, curves = her body the way that it is. She also has to guard against rejecting any person commenting on her appearance. By slowing down and noticing automatic thoughts and emotions in response to any comments about her appearance while also accepting such commentary in the context of a positive, affirming, and supportive consensual romantic relationship, she can begin to unpair her brain's learned connection between comments about her appearance and mistrust of men's motivations.

By repeatedly choosing behaviors in line with this mentality, the conditioning changes, and so does the intensity of shame. Without being committed to this, Stephanie is unlikely to effectively overcome the shame that is hijacking her from attaining her goals. But by acting with behaviors opposite to those that the shame is asking of her ("Wear baggy clothes and don't do your hair, Stephanie"), she not only addresses her situation, but she also learns to reject falsehoods about herself and clarify that her behaviors are not immoral. Furthermore, by using opposite action, she is also practicing the DBT skill of self-validation (covered in more detail in chapter 14), recognizing that she did nothing wrong and that, given how her uncle treated her, it makes sense that she would feel the way she does. For bonus points, Stephanie could generalize her newfound mastery over shame by applying it to her work environment, going out for dinner, spending time with friends, and looking for other ways to defy the connection between being *herself* and being *bad*.

Shame and ERP

Many people struggle with shame in the course of confronting their unwanted thoughts and fears, especially in the context of OCD and related conditions. Thoughts and feelings interact with one another, but psychiatric conditions also interact with one another. If you have OCD or something like it, the condition communicates with BPD and others like it, and this back-and-forth can be a wellspring of shame for the person experiencing it. One common internal discourse we see in clinical practice goes like this:

> You identify a level of exposure for your target fear that you think you can tolerate. It's low on your hierarchy, but it's nonetheless challenging enough to require some effort. You approach the exposure, either by beginning it or getting ready to begin it, but then the back-and-forth interactions start.

> OCD: "You can't do this. It's too scary and all your fears will come true."

> Therapist and/or Wise Mind (TWM): "You got this."

> BPD: "This should be easy, but it isn't because you're weak and ridiculous."

> OCD: "If you do this, you'll regret it."

> TWM: "Remember, doing the hard things is how you get better!"

> BPD: "Who do you think you are to deserve getting better? You're nothing, you're pathetic."

OCD: "This is too much anxiety. You set your exposure too high."

BPD: "This is unbearable anxiety. You're going to crack up. You look insane."

TWM: "What's wrong? Maybe we should try something a bit less intense?"

OCD: "You cannot handle this trigger."

BPD: "You cannot handle life."

If you've experienced anything like this, know that you are not alone. This kind of mental space is hard enough to be in, but it also often comes with the inability to put the experience into words, which can make you feel even worse as the people who care about you struggle to understand what is going on.

When you get stuck in this trance of shame, your best strategy is to stop what you're doing, take a step back, and give yourself some space to recognize that shame is present. Here's a good place for the easy-to-remember STOP skill. Simply pushing shame down only strengthens it, and simply running away from the situation has pretty much the same result. Just as with unwanted thoughts, when you respond to shame like it is dangerous (by forcing it away or running from it), you teach the brain to be threatened by it. Instead, we want the brain to see shame as a manageable part of life, not more powerful than you are. You can bring the shame into the room, call it out, and make it another experience in the body that you can observe arising when you practice ERP.

PRACTICE: Your Experience of Shame

Given everything we've discussed in this chapter, think about your own experience of shame. Which community values do you find most distressing to transgress? *Have* you actually transgressed them? Following the examples provided, use this chart to assess justified versus unjustified shame:

Shame Experience	Justified Have you violated a generally accepted community norm (literally, not theoretically)?	Unjustified Have you violated a generally accepted community norm?
Example: I stole a pair of nice-looking gloves from a neighborhood shop.	X In most communities, stealing, particularly from small mom-and-pop stores, is considered a violation.	
Example: I feel ashamed of my car since it's not as nice as my neighbors' cars.		X In most communities, the quality of your car would not be a violation.
Your example 1:		
Your example 2:		
Your example 3:		

CHAPTER 11

Reflecting Mindfully vs. Self-Criticism

Shaka is a thirty-three-year-old software engineer who left a start-up company two years ago because he was unhappy and unfulfilled at his job and his salary barely covered his monthly costs. He recently read that his old company had gone public—had he stayed, he would have made millions. His current job is much more to his liking, he enjoys the work environment, and he's done well financially, but nothing like how he would have made out if he'd stayed with the start-up.

Now he spends a lot of time ruminating on what could have been and kicking himself for leaving his old job. Every time he sees a sports car, he thinks he could have owned one. His old colleagues are now living in exclusive high-rise condos overlooking the river, and he imagines them traveling all over the world in first class. He's not sleeping well because all he can think about is what he let get away.

He met Amara, the love of his life, at a college reunion soon after leaving the start-up, something he wouldn't have had time to attend at his old job, but he's not ruminating about how lucky he is to be with such a wonderful mate. Instead, he's stuck on the millions he could have made if he'd just stayed a few more years.

Rumination and Regret

We tend to determine that something was a bad decision when the outcomes don't go the way we wanted, ignoring the fact that we made the original choice based on what felt right to us at the time, with the information we had on hand. We all make decisions all the time with imperfect information. You buy a house and you learn later that the septic system isn't up to code. You fall in love with someone and marry them only to discover later that they have an unhealthy addiction. Even when we have a great deal of accurate information and make an absolute decision, not every one will turn out to be the right or best choice for you in retrospect.

It's easy to imagine what might have been, to look back with regret on something we wished we'd done. But rumination makes this a whole lot worse. You may replay a past scenario over and over again in your mind, imagining what you could have done differently. But every moment you spend ruminating on the past is a moment wasted in the present, and before you know it, you're spending your whole life living in a past you regret. Today will be the past tomorrow. Do you really want to devote precious time today and tomorrow to yesterday?

Moving beyond rumination is so important because one of its more troubling aspects is the impact it has on broader functioning, like Shaka's restless sleep. When you're worrying all the time about whatever it is that worries you, it will inevitably affect your relationships, your parenting, your productivity at work, and pretty much everything else in your life. This is compounded rumination, and it's time to do something about it before it takes over your mind and your experience.

Mindfulness vs. Mindlessness

In this stressed-out world, if you do a web search for ways to de-stress, the practice of mindfulness will virtually always appear. We're big advocates of mindfulness and have written widely on the practice, and yet here we want to make a small plug for mindlessness. Research has shown that, for many tasks, it's actually more efficient to be mindless. As we develop skill in complex tasks—for example, driving—we can perform them with increasing ease until attention is almost unnecessary. When a teen first learns to drive, they're hyperaware of every aspect of driving, but once a driver becomes fully competent, they no longer need to stop to think about each and every step. The same is true of most everyday activities, like brushing your teeth, riding a bicycle, or bringing a fork to your mouth—all of which were difficult when you were first learning them.

What allows us to execute behaviors without paying attention to them is stored muscle memory. This memory permits us to engage in repeatedly practiced and learned behaviors automatically, without conscious awareness. That doesn't mean they can't be done mindfully, they just don't need to be done mindfully to be efficient.

Now, there's no question that paying attention is important when learning a new skill, particularly when we want to be proficient in that skill; but once we have learned it, we can let go of such concentrated consciousness and let muscle memory take over. This works to our advantage with some behaviors (you don't have to relearn how to ride a bike each time you get on one), but it works to our disadvantage with certain actions and behaviors that are not good or adaptive for us but have nevertheless entered our muscle memory.

Mindlessness is of very little benefit, for example, when the automatic behavior is rumination. Rumination, which is repetitive, mindless, negative self-focused thinking, can lead to depression, negative mood states, a focus on negative stories, and the recollection of negative memories, like Shaka being stuck in the "what if" of his situation instead of the "what is." Ruminating on what could have been does not change the reality of his situation at all.

Mindlessly beating yourself up, attacking yourself, or living in regret is a misuse of the power of choosing where to put your attention. Rumination typically begins when the results of a goal you set out to achieve are quite different from what you'd hoped for. So, like Shaka, you replay the situation over and over in your head, wondering what went wrong and blaming yourself for the outcome. In turn, rumination negatively impacts your emotions, self-worth, and problem-solving skills and erodes your motivation. Bottom line: there is no upside to rumination.

How to Replace Rumination with Mindful Reflection

So how can you move beyond useless ruminating and get to a healthier, more mindful place? Let's start with what *not* to do, and that is any attempt to suppress your thoughts. You might think that always distracting yourself from negative ruminations will get rid of them, but research shows that thought suppression actually leads to an intensification of the negative thoughts and causes you to ruminate more. The reason for this is that it takes a lot of mental energy to suppress your thoughts, and so when you're in a stressful situation that requires your attention and energy, the repressed thoughts come flooding back into your mind.

In many ways, "suppressing" and "forcing control" of situations have similar outcomes. Not taking control of rumination is similar to not paying attention to a leaking pipe. The other alternative is forcing control by simply plugging the leaking pipe. The problem is that, ultimately, either way, the pipe will burst at some point and the damage will be a lot worse than if you'd dealt with the leak in the first place. The middle path is to recognize that neither avoiding nor forcing is the way to go; instead, it's optimal to get an expert to deal with the situation. If you feel you are either avoiding a situation by suppressing it or forcing a solution that only temporarily fixes the problem, you're likely to make matters worse. There are other alternatives.

Being Effective: Doing What Works

One of the specific mindfulness practices in DBT is to do what is *effective*, meaning focusing on what works rather than on what's "unfair" or what "should have been." Rumination is an ineffective use of thinking. For example, if you don't do well on a test and then spend the next week having negative thoughts about yourself because of that, the endlessly looping thoughts do nothing but get in the way of studying for your next test. You'd do much better to spend that energy on figuring out what went wrong and how you can be better prepared in future. It can feel as if you don't have a choice in rumination, but mindfulness is a powerful tool in using your thoughts effectively.

The Role of Mindfulness in Conquering Rumination

Mindfulness involves paying full attention to the present moment and doing so with intention and without judgment. The present moment encompasses everything, including the thoughts in your head, some of which can be distressing and painful, particularly those you're ruminating on. Asking you to not avoid them but instead mindfully observe them, we realize, can be the exact opposite of what you want to do. But when you use mindfulness effectively, you shift your focus away from ideas of fairness and unfairness, of who is right and who is wrong, and instead focus on what the situation needs. Say you run over a pothole and get a flat tire. You didn't make the pothole or the tire, but blaming your town's public works department or the tire manufacturer is not the effective thing to do. What the situation calls for is for you to change the tire and get to work.

How Does Mindfulness Target Rumination?

1. Mindfulness directs your attention to the present experience. It shifts your attention from the past or future to the present, which interrupts ruminating because the past and future situations are not happening right now.

2. Mindfulness emphasizes the practice of self-acceptance and self-compassion. *Self-acceptance* is working toward observing yourself as a whole, with all your strengths and flaws. It can often feel like others have only strengths, but every one of us has weaknesses. Once you accept them, you can decide whether you are going to work on changing them or if you're okay with them. *Self-compassion* is slightly different in that it includes the goal of alleviating your suffering and, as such, is a powerful motivating force for actively pursuing growth and change. Both of these qualities can help you combat the negative self-assessment that arises from rumination.

3. Mindfulness cultivates a recognition about the way you think and, in turn, protects you against overidentifying with negative states. Rumination is one of these states.

It helps to recognize that nothing is permanent, not even thoughts that seem ceaseless. By seeing your thoughts as temporary phenomena, you can let them show up and then pass through your mind without engaging with them and without allowing the content of them to define you. The more you practice mindfulness, the less sensitive you'll be to negative thoughts; as a result, they become less relevant and so you ruminate less.

PRACTICE: A Specific Mindfulness Practice

Everything we do mindlessly we can do mindfully. So let's do a mindfulness exercise involving an every-day, usually mindless activity. When practicing mindfulness, you may notice that your mind wanders to other thoughts—this is a common experience and, just like ruminations, the thoughts will pass. So when you notice them, simply notice them without judgment and go back to the mindfulness activity. In this example, you can drink a cup of tea mindlessly while watching the news or talking on the phone, or you can drink it mindfully by following these steps:

1. **Choose.** Intentionally make a choice that you feel captures your present moment. Not every kind of tea fits every occasion. Perhaps opt for chamomile if it's close to bedtime or black tea to start your day.

2. **Listen.** Boil the water and really listen to it. Whether you use a kettle or a microwave, intention-ally listen to the sound of the water heating or the microwave whirring until the ding. While you wait, don't distract with the radio or your phone—just sit and listen.

3. **Watch.** Fill your cup with water. Notice how the water changes color as it comes into contact with the tea. Watch as the color becomes deeper and darker as the tea and hot water blend.

4. **Smell.** Spend a few moments of your in-breath smelling the aromas of the tea steeping.

5. **Feel and taste.** As you bring the cup to your lips, feel the warmth of the tea and then sip slowly and notice the flavor.

But Wait, There's More Mindfulness!

There are other things you can do—anytime, anywhere—to make mindfulness more a part of your daily life, such as:

- **Practice breath awareness:** bring all your attention to the breath and follow it from the moment you start your inhale to the moment you finish your exhale.

- **Do a body scan or progressive muscle relaxation exercise** (see chapter 7 for an example).

- **Anchor your attention:** listen to a song or take in a painting and make just one element (like the bass line or the brushstrokes) the anchor of your attention.

- **Practice mindful walking:** for five minutes, engage in very slow, deliberate, and inten-tional walking that brings attention to every element of the stepping process.

- **Make up your own mindfulness exercise or game:** a mindfulness activity is really *any*thing that invites you to pay attention to one thing and return your attention to that thing whenever you become aware that your mind has wandered away—be inventive and have fun!

Taking Responsibility for Where You Put Your Focus

Let's go back to Shaka for a moment. He's beating himself up with regret that he didn't stay at his former job longer to make millions of dollars. Playing these thoughts over and over again in his head is the very definition of rumination. Whether he recognizes it or not, he actually has a choice over where he directs his attention, and it is his responsibility to make that choice.

If he's going to ruminate on the past, then he can do so mindfully by bringing his attention to his ruminations, yes, but then adding more thoughts to those thoughts that are equally true and valid for him. He has no idea where he'd be right now, for example, if he'd stayed. He likely would never have met his girlfriend, and he certainly wouldn't have the job he's enjoyed for the last two years, but maybe the stress of the old job would have been too much for him. He could have a nicer car and a plush apartment, sure, but he also might have burnt out. Or the start-up could have gone under. Or his bosses, noticing his unhappiness there, could have let him go before the big payout. The point is, we can never know the outcome of anything until it actually happens, but we can proactively choose to concentrate on the present moment and make the best decisions we can within it.

PRACTICE: Your Experience of Mindful Responses vs. Self-Attack

Think about a situation in your own life that has caused you excessive regret. Using the chart below, how can you reframe your shame and self-criticism into a more mindful response to the situation?

Rumination	Self-Attack	Mindful Response	Integrated View
For Shaka: I lost so much money leaving that job!	I'm a loser for giving up millions of dollars.	I've been in a job that I love for the past two years.	Having more money would have made my life easier in some ways, yet I wouldn't have found this job I love.

Rumination	Self-Attack	Mindful Response	Integrated View
For Shaka: I'm so stupid for leaving my job.	All my former colleagues were smarter than me for staying.	I met the person I want to spend the rest of my life with.	My former coworkers are doing well, and yet without leaving, I wouldn't have met my partner.
Your example 1:			
Your example 2:			

Self-Criticism and Compulsion

There's nothing wrong with looking back on your experiences and asking what you've learned from them. Self-reflection can be a healthy, even mindful way of making sense of things. But how can something be mindful and past-oriented at the same time? Here's how: by being aware in the present of what you are doing with intention—looking back on your past to see it for what it really was and is. Mindless rumination, or the endless looping in your head of all your mistakes, is something altogether different.

Many people find their intrusive thoughts to be more than just scary, but offensive, taboo, or otherwise unacceptable. The same is true of thoughts about the past. You might look at some choice you made or some missed opportunity and think, *How stupid must I have been?* Though this is normal to some extent, it is still fundamentally ineffective. Self-reflection is done mindfully, with curiosity and with an eye to learning. Name-calling and other forms of self-criticism may seem like opportunities for growth, but they're really just compulsions: an act designed to even the score, so to speak. If you have an obsession about contamination, your compulsion will be to excessively wash. If you have an obsession about being a failure of a human being, the compulsion will be to make sure you've been adequately punished.

Self-reflection is a healthy exploration of how we can make wise choices moving forward, but self-criticism takes us further into pointless confusion. You can easily tell the difference between the two by identifying the purpose of the mental behavior. Are you trying to learn something, or are you trying to cause yourself pain? Self-criticism and self-punishment always say the same thing: *I should have known better than to end up here.* But if you're paying attention, this claim makes no sense. How could you have known better?

Every step along the way, you can only do the best you can with what you have, and that includes skills and knowledge. And where do skills and knowledge come from? They come from your lived experiences. You don't choose your genetics, your parents, the country or culture in which you were born. What you choose exists only in this moment—where you choose to direct your attention and whether you strive to apply it skillfully or toward beating yourself up.

To conclude this chapter on the distinction between beating yourself up or building your self-acceptance, try this for practice:

Self-Criticism	Purpose Why do you tell yourself this?	Self-Reflection	Purpose How is this helpful to you?
I made a dumb choice.	I deserve to feel bad.	I made a choice that didn't produce the desired results. I can make a more effective choice next time.	I would like to learn from my experience.
I'm a failure of a human being because of my OCD.	I hate myself for having OCD symptoms.	I'm having a hard time standing up to my OCD, and I could reach out for more tools and support.	I want to develop mastery over my OCD and be less impaired by it.

Self-Criticism	Purpose Why do you tell yourself this?	Self-Reflection	Purpose How is this helpful to you?

CHAPTER 12

Self-Compassion vs. Making Excuses

Erica hit snooze one too many times and was late for work. Her manager reprimanded her in front of the whole department and docked her pay. After spending most of the day giving herself a hard time for being so stupid, she remembered to apply some self-compassion to the equation. She'd messed up. Okay, accept it and move on. Maybe put the alarm on the other side of the room so she'd have to get up to turn it off? That could help.

But then a competing voice in her head had trouble accepting responsibility. Why couldn't her manager cut her a little slack? She wouldn't have been late if she didn't need more sleep, which was due to working too hard in the first place! As she stewed over all this, dissatisfaction with her boss, her job, her financial situation, and pretty much everything in her life continued to mount.

Erica gets off on the right foot, trying to treat herself with kindness after making an embarrassing mistake, but when dealing with the consequences of this mistake, she turns to thoughts of blaming others. This may feel like self-kindness, but it only ends up filling her with unnecessary painful emotions that chip away at her mood and clarity about the situation. So if we understand the futility of self-criticism (see the previous chapter), how do we strike a balance between being kind to ourselves while also being objective about accountability for our choices?

A big part of this challenge is zeroing in on the answer to the question: What would be helpful now? We may think assigning blame is helpful because it relieves us of short-term discomfort, but ultimately, it isn't helpful to the problem at hand. You made a mistake of some kind—you had an inappropriate thought or feeling, you hurt someone's feelings, you made others worry about you, you behaved in a way contrary to your values—and just giving yourself a metaphorical hug with self-kindness doesn't seem any more adequate than making excuses. What would be helpful is to figure out a way to take ownership of your experience without being self-abusive.

A frequent source of confusion is the idea that showing self-kindness or self-compassion is the same thing as being "nice." Self-kindness is about treating yourself like you would a loved one. But we don't always treat our loved ones "nicely" even when we are treating them with love and kindness, right? For example, if you have a loved one who is struggling with drug addiction, you might be quite direct in how you discourage them from unhealthy behavior and encourage them to seek help. You could be kind about this—validating how hard it is, acknowledging how much you wish them not to suffer—but you may not necessarily be nice or even gentle about it.

Kindness is grounded in the desire for reduced suffering, and there are many ways to get there. A good athletic coach doesn't say, "Just have fun—you all get trophies, anyway, so who cares?" The coach says, "I believe in you—now get out there and hustle!" If your obsessive mind is being cruel to you, it's okay to tell yourself to shut up, so long as the tone is directed toward being helpful. Sometimes your best friend needs a punch in the arm and a "stop being ridiculous" comment when you see them going on and on about how terrible they are. You can turn this same "tough love" inward.

In CBT, thought records can be useful for teasing apart what is and isn't helpful. Recall from earlier in the book that challenging distorted thoughts separates the false problem (trying to be certain about the future or change the past) from the real problem (coping with a challenging emotion or uncertainty in the present moment). The same skill can be used to separate self-kindness from avoiding responsibility—try it now on this simplified version of the thought record chart in chapter 3:

Trigger	False Project or Automatic Thought	Real Project or Thought Challenge
Overslept	Not my fault, work is too early.	I screwed up and am not happy about it, but I don't have to be perfect and I can put the alarm on the other side of the room. Ruminating and beating myself up won't help me avoid this discomfort next time.

Many people are hesitant to invest in self-compassion because it feels like cheating somehow. In actuality, self-compassion is the best way to take responsibility for situations in which you may have been unskillful and therefore have an opportunity to learn from. You may be thinking, *Okay, but how do I know for sure that I'm taking enough responsibility for what I've done and not just being nice to myself to let myself off easy for being a jerk?* This might be a good opportunity to practice your ERP skills, shrug, and move forward with the possibility.

List some situations in which you can benefit from being kind to yourself:

_____

_____

_____

_____

What would be helpful to ensure you are still taking responsibility for yourself while also being kind to yourself?

_____

_____

_____

_____

Checking In

Well, that brings us to the end of the second part of the book, which hopefully clarified some of the nuances of working with unwanted thoughts and difficult emotions. We've covered a lot of skills either explicitly or in summary, but don't worry about memorizing or mastering them just yet. In the next section of this book, we'll give you a chance to practice applying these tools (and in the final chapter, we'll pull them all together for you in one place).

But before jumping into part 3, give yourself a break. Stop "working on yourself" for a bit and just be a person with thoughts and feelings who doesn't need to fix or change things right now. You've earned it.

Putting the Tools to Use

Welcome to the final part of our book! In the first part, we described the way ERP and DBT each work to address the problem of navigating unwanted thoughts and feelings. In the second part, we looked at specific interactions between thoughts and feelings, where a combined approach can be most useful. This part is where we get lazy and have you do the rest of the work! Well, sort of.

In the pages ahead, we present a template for making *you* the center of your own "case study" by looking at five specific areas where people tend to struggle with dysregulation. In this way, you can collect the unwanted thoughts and challenging emotions you'd like to work on, then connect them to the most useful CBT, ERP, and DBT tools for you. Sure, part of our strategy here is avoiding the uncomfortable position of telling you what to do; after all, we haven't met you and can't possibly know the details of your situation nearly as well as you do. So by positioning you as the expert of your experience, then adding guidance we've gleaned from our clinical backgrounds, the next chapter will hopefully allow you to create a roadmap for a life lived joyfully.

We'll then proceed to a discussion of self-validation, an extremely important concept for taking command of your mental health journey. In the final chapter, we'll review all the core concepts in one place in the form of a handy reference guide.

CHAPTER 13

Choose Your Own Mental Health Plan of Action

We're going to take a look now at five ways in which people tend to experience dysregulation—that is, feeling thrown off by their thoughts and feelings. Each section presents a narrative of a person experiencing a particular kind of dysregulation (we hope that person is you and we hope the story therefore resonates, so feel free to substitute any words or thoughts that will make it more relevant to you). We've purposely left out certain parts of each narrative so you can fill in the blanks, inserting your own wisdom about which tools are likely to be the most effective for your specific challenges. Take anything you want from any part of this book to fill in the blanks. We've included corresponding tips for each numbered section. There is no "wrong" way to do this; it's just a means to craft a personalized treatment plan that addresses the ways in which your thoughts and feelings cause you difficulty.

Your Case Example #1: Emotion Dysregulation

I can be an emotionally intense person. Life seems to be so much more vivid for me than it is for other people. People consider me empathic, sensitive, perceptive, and creative. Sometimes this is great, but sometimes it's a liability. When things are going well, emotional intensity comes with

1. _____

_____.

[insert your experience of intense positive emotions]

At their worst, intense emotions feel like _____

_____.

[insert your experience of intense negative emotions]

2. There are certain situations that make me feel _____

_____,

[insert your emotions here]

and this in turn can make me do _____

_____.

[insert behavior that might be problematic here]

3. When that shows up, especially if I catch it early enough, I can use _____

_____

[insert tool here]

to help me reduce the level of intensity of the emotion and root out distorted thinking. 4. But when I get flooded by the intensity of the emotion, it can be useful to bring in _____

_____

[insert tool here]

to make my emotions more tolerable. Sometimes when I'm especially upset, I am at risk of not only

_____

_____,

[insert behavior here]

but perhaps even making the situation worse by _____

_____.

[insert behavior that could make things worse in the long run]

5. So by practicing _____,

[insert skillful practice]

I can regain my emotional balance and be more effective.

Guidance

In filling out the above template, you may find this guidance useful:

1. Different emotions can lead to different types of behaviors. Some of these behaviors are exactly what the situation calls for and others make the situation worse, even if they feel good in the moment. The level of the emotion also plays a role in how behavior is displayed. For instance, you might be someone who ignores another person if you are mildly irritated by them, but yells and insults that person if you are furious at them. Before acting on any emotion, you may want to distance yourself from the situation, explore and name the specific emotion, decide if it is primary or secondary (see chapter 2), validate the emotion, determine whether it is justified or not, *then* decide what to do. Use the narrative above to identify which emotions are most problematic for you, what brings them on, and how they impact you in the short and the long term.

2. Emotions can be particularly intense when brought on by interpersonal conflict; however, they can also be brought on by *intra*personal conflict, meaning that the thoughts you have about yourself can lead to intense emotions. You might reflect on the thoughts described in chapter 1 to bring to mind which ones you're experiencing. It can be helpful to also describe how they manifest in your body and what it's like to be in the presence of these emotions, both when they are and are not manageable and when they are prompted by your relationship with someone else or by your own thoughts.

3. This is where you can identify the most effective tools for catching overpowering emotions that can make your experience seem unbearable. Identifying and challenging those emotions before they become an emotional tsunami might come in handy here. Opposite action may be particularly useful, or you might use an automatic thought record to challenge how you're thinking about your experience.

4. If your intense emotions are unwanted and painful, then first using a DBT distress tolerance skill and then using longer-term emotion regulation skills is likely the way to go. Here, you might make a list of specific emotions and then specific distress tolerance skills that are effective in your situation. If something works well, you can use that regularly, or you can experiment with other ideas, such as mindfulness, that can also be helpful.

5. Even if you are struggling with naming and labeling your emotion, you can still use various skills. What DBT strategies have you encountered in this book that could be your go-to tools when things feel overwhelming? Perhaps an ice dive or paced breathing or sprinting around the block. Consider precisely when and how you would use your preferred tool and what you would do instead if you were not in a situation to use that tool.

Your Case Example #2: Interpersonal Dysregulation

I really value my relationship with _____.

[insert name of person here]

1. However, sometimes thoughts about the relationship cause me distress, such as _____

_____

_____.

[insert thoughts here:]

2. These thoughts about the relationship sometimes bring on intense feelings of _____

_____.

[insert feelings here]

3. When I'm worried about the relationship, I can use _____

_____

[insert tool here]

to help me root out distorted thinking. 4. I can also do exposure to my fearful thoughts about the relationship by _____

_____.

[insert tool here]

5. But when I get overwhelmed by it all, it can be really useful to bring in _____

_____

[insert tool here]

to make my emotions more tolerable. 6. Sometimes when I'm especially upset, I want to communicate to the person in this relationship what's going on, and I can use _____

_____

[insert tool here]

to make it more likely that this communication will be effective.

Guidance

In filling out the above template, you may find this guidance useful:

1. Different types of relationships can bring on a wide array of unwanted thoughts, especially if you have a tendency to love others with intensity and struggle when you feel too connected or not connected enough to another person. Sometimes people struggle with the thought that they are not loved or appreciated as much as they love and appreciate the other person. Sometimes people struggle with the thought that the relationship is not ideal, that the other person may not be "the one," or that they don't have the "right" feelings for them. Some people struggle with themes of trust in relationships and have unwanted thoughts about being cheated on, manipulated, disrespected, or abandoned. Look back to chapter 1 to explore what types of thoughts come up for you categorically (catastrophic, taboo, self-critical, judgmental), and use the space above to identify which specific thoughts bring on distress in your relationship.

2. Feelings around relationships can be very intense for those predisposed to emotional reactivity. You might reflect on the feelings described in chapter 2 to bring to mind which ones you're experiencing. It can be helpful to also describe how they manifest in your body and what it's like for you to be in the presence of these feelings.

3. This is where you can identify the most effective tools for you when it comes to catching distorted thinking that can make your experience seem intolerable. Identifying and challenging cognitive distortions might come in handy here, as well as the automatic thought record.

4. If your thoughts about the relationship are unwanted and intrusive, then you might treat them as obsessions, in which case, exposure-based tools could be effective. Consider whether this is something to which you can apply in vivo exposure, imaginal exposure, or interoceptive exposure. How might you organize these exposures into a hierarchy and practice them until your fears seem more manageable? How can you identify and resist avoidance, reassurance, and other compulsions that might be giving unwanted thoughts their power?

5. With or without the added stressor of trying to confront your fears, emotions around interpersonal dysregulation (that is, feeling unsafe or unstable in the context of a relationship with another person) can be very intense. What DBT strategies can serve as your go-to tools when things feel truly out of control? Perhaps a body scan or one of the steps in the TIPP skill is the most effective for you. Precisely when and how would you use this tool?

6. Trying to be heard and understood in the midst of being dysregulated in a relationship is really hard. Which strategies make the most sense for you when your goal is to communicate your needs clearly to another person?

Your Case Example #3: Behavioral Dysregulation

1. I feel that I can manage most things in my life, but at times, when _____

_____

_____

[insert unwanted thought, intense emotion, or other difficult circumstance here]

shows up, I have a hard time coping. 2. That's when I typically turn to the behavior of _____

_____.

[insert behavior that may help or feel good at first, but is problematic or harmful]

3. The truth is, this behavior doesn't help me cope as much as it helps me temporarily escape from my distress. I can tell because _____

_____.

[insert how this behavior does not actually support you in the long run]

Just because I know there are consequences to these behaviors doesn't mean they're going to stop on their own. 4. I can motivate myself to change these behaviors by remembering all the benefits of resisting them, such as _____

_____.

[insert what you get in return for resisting harmful behaviors]

But just knowing that won't be enough. I have to be able to navigate those unwanted thoughts and feelings that keep pushing me to fall back on problem behaviors. 5. I can use skills like _____

_____

[insert DBT and ERP skills here]

to point me in a wiser direction.

Guidance

In filling out the above template, you may find this guidance useful:

1. Consider the types of unwanted thoughts or difficult emotions or situations that reliably throw you off-balance. This could be an intrusive ego-dystonic thought, such as an OCD obsession, or it could be an ego-syntonic thought, such as a self-criticism of your appearance or self-worth. It could be an emotion you find especially hard to navigate, such as fear or shame. Or perhaps these unwanted thoughts and feelings are tied to specific events, such as social gatherings or work challenges.

2. There's a difference between behaviors that are helpful in the short run and those that are helpful in the long run. Some seem helpful in the short run and turn out not to be, and others just feel good but are immediately harmful—self-injury, bingeing, purging, substance abuse, acting aggressively toward others, and engaging in impairing rituals or compulsions fit into this category. If you have a tendency to act without thinking, particularly when your emotions are strong, you really want to pay attention to this because you are at risk of repeating potentially unhelpful behaviors with potentially increasingly negative outcomes.

3. Recall the distinction made in chapter 6 between coping and compulsing. Coping strategies help us navigate difficult thoughts and emotions, whereas compulsions (and other maladaptive behaviors) simply dull, suppress, or unskillfully distract from them. How is your behavior getting in the way of actually developing mastery over this challenge? What additional problems develop from these behaviors (like having to apologize for hurting someone or having to hide the evidence of self-injury)?

4. Consider what your world actually looks like when you refrain from unhealthy behaviors or detrimental compulsions. What do your relationships look like? How does your body feel? What other wanted changes arise in your life?

5. One tool to use for catching the triggers that lead to problem behaviors is simply to keep a written record of them. Basically, you'd reverse engineer what happened to lead you to choose an unhelpful behavior so you can determine how you got there. Then, you can identify which skills could help you make different choices next time: a cognitive skill like a thought record, an emotion regulation skill like TIPP, a mindfulness skill like STOP, or an exposure-based skill. What DBT tools that you've encountered in this book can you employ when you feel you're going to act on problem behaviors?

Your Case Example #4: Cognitive Dysregulation

1. I have unwanted intrusive thoughts, like _____

_____

_____.

[insert thoughts here]

2. When something triggers them or when they just pop in my head, I feel _____

_____.

[insert feelings]

3. I try to get the thoughts to go away with compulsions like _____

_____.

[insert compulsions]

In the moment, it just seems so important to do these compulsions. 4. It can be helpful to recognize when my thinking is distorted on this subject by using _____

_____

[insert tools]

5. or by doing exposures to them in the form of _____

_____.

[insert tools]

But sometimes, I just really hate that I have these thoughts and really believe I must be some kind of terrible person for even thinking them. 6. Using _____

_____

[insert tools]

can help me treat myself better when I'm in that space.

Guidance

In filling out the above template, you may find this guidance useful:

1. Whether they are brought on by OCD, social anxiety, PTSD, or just life, intrusive thoughts can be shocking, frustrating, and painful. In chapter 1, we asked you to write down some of your troubling thoughts. Here is another opportunity to just put them into words in front of you so you can see what they are (literally, just words in your head!).

2. When thoughts attack, they can quickly stir up a variety of challenging emotions. Anxiety, disgust, or anger may be predominant, but other emotions may show up as well. Take another look at the emotions you explored in chapter 2 and see which apply the most to dealing with your unwanted thoughts.

3. It can be useful here to do a quick inventory of all the ways you try to get certain about your unwanted thoughts or try to make the associated feelings go away. Remember that these are not coping strategies that allow you to tolerate or embrace the feelings; they are compulsions or rituals aimed at escaping them.

4. Cognitive restructuring tools like those described in chapter 3 can be useful for catching and modifying distorted thinking. Or you might try just mindfully recognizing the thinking style that is leading you astray and make a short list of your cognitive distortions.

5. If you're going to use ERP strategies to address your unwanted thoughts, consider the different ways you might incorporate in vivo, imaginal, or interoceptive exposures. You might include some details about how you would approach exposures hierarchically or how you might pace the frequency and intensity of your exposures. Alternatively, you can use this space to simply acknowledge things you might start doing again that you've been avoiding, knowing that they'll bring on the thoughts but that they'll also be rewarding.

6. Self-judgmental thoughts can be brutal, and sometimes we end up responding to our original triggering thoughts with compulsions just to avoid dealing with the self-hating thoughts that show up when we try to navigate them at all. Here, you might identify some DBT skills, self-compassion strategies, or other coping mechanisms that are productive for you and keep you in a healthy, therapeutic stance with your thoughts.

Your Case Example #5: Self-Dysregulation

I struggle with knowing who I am; I feel that I change from one moment to the next. I am uncertain as to my abilities. 1. One moment, I feel that I am good at _____

_____,

[insert something you feel skilled at doing here]

and the next moment, I begin to question my abilities. 2. Instead of questioning my abilities, I can engage in

_____

_____.

[insert skills here]

3. I also question my sense of self when I have thoughts of _____

_____.

[insert intrusive thoughts here as well as what you fear these thoughts tell you about yourself]

4. Instead of dwelling on these thoughts, I can use the skills of _____

_____.

[insert skills here]

5. My sense of self is stronger when I work toward my life goals of _____

_____,

[insert goals here]

but when I have strong emotions, my goals begin to shift. 6. Instead of changing my life goals, I can

_____

_____.

[insert skills you can use]

Guidance

In filling out the above template, you may find this guidance useful:

1. Insight is an important first step in figuring out what you want to do, but insight alone is not enough. People who smoke have the insight that smoking is unhealthy, and yet this doesn't typically stop them from smoking. For accurate descriptors of who you are, the observation and description skills inherent in mindfulness are excellent tools to use.

2. When you begin to question yourself and your capabilities, this can lead to significant self-doubt and emotional distress. Are your doubts valid? Check the facts (chapter 6). Are your emotions justified? Use emotion regulation skills (chapter 4) to determine if your emotions are justified or not and to then help you decide how to deal with them.

3. Writing down your thoughts and fears is a powerful technique to reduce the grip they have over your life. Just putting down in words something that feels bigger than you can handle can make it easier to handle. The key is to just state the facts of your experience. If you have a thought, label it as just a thought. Unless a thought leads to an action, it remains a thought. Make sure you're not equating the thoughts you have with who you are as a person.

4. As in the previous case example, if you're going to use ERP strategies to address your unwanted thoughts, consider the ways you can incorporate in vivo, imaginal, or interoceptive exposures. Alternatively, you can apply the DBT skill of acceptance to your unwanted thoughts, even incorporating an element of irreverence, laughing at the thought as if to say, *There you go again, mind!* Recognize that what you think is not who you are.

5. Mindfulness is the most useful skill for determining your goals. If it is a specific goal—such as "I want to be a nurse"—write it down, make a poster, and tape it to your wall. If it is a general goal—"I want to help people"—mindfulness will help narrow down the course of study or employment field you want to pursue.

6. If intense emotions and unwanted thoughts are derailing the path to your goals, this is not the time to give up. You may need to slow down for a bit, but keep your eyes on the proverbial prize. Using emotion regulation skills to address emotional excess and ERP skills to handle unwanted and unhelpful thoughts will steer you back on track. And consider asking for help. Talking to people who know and love you, those with whom you have shared your values and goals, will also help you stay on track. If you do ask for help, make sure it's for wise reasons. In other words, make sure you're not simply seeking reassurance, because that will only keep you depending on others for decision-making instead of strengthening your sense of self.

CHAPTER 14

The Power of Validation

At the core of every challenge we've aimed to address in this book is one central message: your experience is real. Let's be crystal clear here. We are not saying that your unwanted thoughts are going to come true or that all of your feelings are justified all of the time. We are saying that whatever you are experiencing, that is your experience of it and it is the reality you are in. Any other person in your shoes would have to face those same thoughts, feel that same pain and fear, and come up with a strategy for responding to it all. You are not crazy or wrong for having thoughts and feelings that those around you may not be aware of, experience themselves, or understand. You are allowed to be you with whatever thoughts and feelings arise, and that is a valid way to be.

Before we talk about the super-skill of validation, let's review the concept of *invalidation* because we've found that it lies at the root of much mental illness and psychological distress. There are two types of invalidation: an invalidating environment and your own self-invalidation.

An invalidating environment is one in which your communication of private and personal experiences is met with dismissal, trivialization, or punishment. In other words, how you feel and think is not recognized as having validity; instead, it is rejected. The experience of painful emotions, as well as the factor(s) that caused the emotional pain, is disregarded. Invalidation essentially negates or dismisses emotions, thoughts, and behaviors independent of their legitimacy. This can then lead to the second form of invalidation, which is when you invalidate yourself. You think, *If the world is telling me my experiences are wrong or people are punishing or disregarding how I feel, then my thoughts and feelings can't be right.*

Invalidation has four primary features:

1. It tells you that you are wrong in both your description and your assessment of your own experiences, particularly in your perspective of what is causing your emotions, beliefs, and actions. For example, you might feel sad about moving away from a friend and your parents tell you that she was not such a good friend and that people move all the time and that you should just get over it.

2. It attributes your experiences to socially unacceptable characteristics of who you are, your personality. "If you were not such a sensitive person, you wouldn't be so sad for such a long time" or "You just need to adopt a positive attitude, that's what your problem is." Another version of this is when behaviors with unintended negative consequences for other people in your life are attributed to intentionally hostile or manipulative reasons: "You're just being extra sad for attention" or "Your fake depression made you take too long to get ready, and now we're late."

3. It tells you that emotional problems are easy to solve: "Don't be so sad that you're leaving your friend" or "Whenever I'm sad, I just go for a walk and get it out of my system."

4. It rewards others in your environment for having the ability to control their emotions: "Isn't your brother so wonderful for knowing how to control himself?"

The bottom line is that invalidation is hurtful. The way to overcome it is to practice the skill of validation and then, ultimately, of self-validation.

What Is Validation in DBT?

Validation is a key concept in DBT. To validate means to recognize the valid aspects of what another person is saying or feeling or the way in which they are behaving. Validation is important for many reasons:

- It demonstrates that you are listening and trying to see the other person's point of view.

- It shows that you are accepting the other person with care and compassion, and as a consequence, it improves relationships.

- It bypasses the battle of who's right and who's wrong and thus reduces defensiveness and anger.

- It lessens the intensity of emotions (since we all tend to feel more emotionally stable when we feel heard), which in turn leads to more effective problem solving.

When people first hear of the concept of validation in DBT, they worry that it means you should agree with or approve of anything another person does. It does not. All it means is that you get where another person is coming from, finding even the smallest amount of truth in their perspective. One of the authors of this book, Blaise, is a strict vegetarian—he believes in the idea of doing no harm to other sentient beings as a value. He does not agree with eating meat, and yet all his family members readily eat meat. He can accept that they enjoy eating meat without having to eat it himself or deviate from his value system. The other author, Jon, grew up on a cattle farm and really appreciates cooking and sharing different beef recipes. The cooking is a mindful awareness practice to him as he takes in all the visuals, smells, and flavors of the experience. Half the people in his house are vegetarian. He can accept that they have no interest in eating meat and understands their reasons why as he also continues to enjoy meat himself.

Validation is neither agreement with nor endorsing a different point of view; instead, it is recognizing that others come to their reality in ways that make their experience valid. An important aspect of validation is that we only validate that which is valid. Asking someone to validate that you failed a test before the results are in would not be validation, and if the other person complied, they would be validating the invalid.

So what things are reliably valid?

- Emotions are always valid. This does *not* mean that they are always justified, that the *reason* for an emotion is necessarily valid, but the emotions themselves as they arise are valid. In other words, whatever emotions you are experiencing at any given moment are what they are—they are your reality. Think about how it feels when you're sad or irritated and someone tells you that's not what you're feeling or that you shouldn't be feeling that way. Does such a statement help? The person doesn't need to agree with you or think your feeling is justified, but it *is* what you are feeling.

- Facts are valid—facts of a situation, of a person's experiences, of their belief systems. For example, if you are Catholic and your friend is Jewish, you don't have to believe in what they believe in just to validate the fact of their faith. People show up in this world however they show up, and that is the reality of their experience whether you think it would be better for them to show up differently or not.

Why Is Validation So Hard Sometimes?

Validation can be difficult to do if you've never done it before. Many people worry that by validating someone when they are upset, that will reinforce them being upset. This is actually the opposite of what happens. By recognizing that someone is upset, it actually helps them calm down. People don't like being upset, and when you let them know that you get it, it helps settle them.

On the other hand, telling someone they're not feeling what they're feeling is likely to make them more upset. When someone you care about is upset, you should express validation, but in a controlled and regulated way—you can express that you understand they are suffering without becoming overwhelmed yourself.

What Is Self-Validation?

Okay, we've talked a bit about validating others, but what about validating yourself? This is even harder for some people to do, particularly if they don't feel they deserve validation. It's wonderful when others validate your experience, but it's even more powerful if you can learn to validate yourself.

Self-validation is a distinctive skill that focuses on accepting the thoughts and emotions you are experiencing as valid—as legit, authentic, credible. Important to remember here is that if you're someone who has difficulty regulating your emotions, you may be prone to reject your struggles or judge yourself for having strong emotions. If you have a difficult time controlling your emotions, you will have a difficult time accepting them.

Self-validation means that when you feel sad or angry about something that happened to you, you don't automatically tell yourself, *I shouldn't feel like this, I'm making a big deal out of the situation.* It means knowing that your past experiences and present situation are real and are part of the reason you're feeling what you're feeling. Similarly, if you're struggling with intrusive thoughts, it simply doesn't work to tell yourself you shouldn't have those thoughts. A self-validating action would be to recognize that you are a person who gets bothered by unwanted thoughts and to acknowledge that this is one of those times when it's happening.

How Do You Self-Validate?

You can begin by using mindfulness to recognize how you are feeling right now and what thoughts are bouncing around in your head. Don't argue with them or try to figure them out, just notice them. At any given time, you can notice how your body feels and identify the emotions you are experiencing.

Here's a process you can follow when you want to seek validation instead of invalidating what you're experiencing:

Step 1: Acknowledge. Simply note and name the emotion you are experiencing in the moment, without judging it. If you feel sad, instead of saying to yourself, *I'm always sad and don't know how to deal with sadness,* simply state the facts: *I am feeling sad right now.* If unwanted thoughts are part of the experience, acknowledge that as well, again without judgment: *I am having a thought about …*

Step 2: Accept. Allow yourself to experience your emotion and know that it's okay to have that emotion. You are permitted to feel whatever you feel—it's simply what you are feeling, even if others don't feel the way you do. Say things to yourself like:

- *This is how I'm feeling right now.*
- *It's okay to feel the way I do.*

- *Just because I feel this way doesn't mean I have to behave destructively.*

- *I know this will pass, but for now, it's how I'm feeling.*

- *I have experienced strong emotions before. I don't like how I'm feeling, but it won't hurt me.*

- *I've had this thought before and there's nothing I need to figure out.*

- *All thoughts come and go, and right now, this is the thought I'm aware of.*

Step 3: Contextualize. Not everyone stops to try to understand why they feel the way they do. So take some time to reflect on how you got to this point, in the context of your overall life, including acknowledging the past events that led you to your present journey. Again, no judging, just considering the objective facts that created the situation you are in right now. Invalidation would have you say, *I have no right to feel sad about what happened because my own stupidity got me into this situation* or *This exposure shouldn't be this hard—I'm never going to overcome this fear.* Those are not the facts; those are judgments. Validation would have you say, *It's understandable that I feel sad. I asked someone to go on a date and they didn't show up. I tend to think people will reject me, so it's no surprise that I feel this way.* Or, *It's okay that I got triggered. I've been struggling with this thought content for some time, and today I'm feeling tired, so it's upsetting.*

PRACTICE: Now it's your turn to practice the steps.

Step 1: **Acknowledge.** Right now, I feel _____.

Step 2: **Accept.** This feels _____, and yet right now, it is what it is.

Step 3: **Contextualize.** I am feeling _____ because

I _____. I am not going to judge myself for this, because

_____. I don't need to make life harder than it is by judging myself; instead,

I can _____.

Once you can self-validate for more manageable emotions, you'll want to apply this to stronger emotions. In preparation, think about a past event where you experienced overwhelming emotions, then consider how you would apply these three steps to that difficult situation.

We near the end of the book on this note for good reason. This is a self-help workbook, meaning you, the reader, have come to it to learn how to help yourself. If you approach your unwanted thoughts and difficult emotions by thinking you shouldn't be experiencing them, then it is unlikely you will show up for yourself when you need to the most. Your human experience is valid. No matter what diagnosis, personality traits, or history you bring with you, your human experience is valid.

To change the way we relate to challenging thoughts and feelings takes tremendous courage. It can feel lonely in mind and body. So your ability to position yourself as someone worth fighting for—someone who's doing the best they can with what they've got, someone who has the capacity to learn and evolve—is the most valuable skill in this book.

CHAPTER 15

Everything in One Place

In the first part of this book, we looked at a wide variety of tools people use to handle unwanted thoughts and challenging emotions. Not every tool works for every person and certainly not for every circumstance, but here we'd like to offer you a simple resource for what tends to go well with what. Much like a recipe for a meal, certain ingredients complement others for the desired effect, so here we've compiled the ingredients for well-being.

CBT and ERP Tools

These strategies are presented in chapter 3, along with their associated worksheets and exercises.

Tool	Function
Identify Cognitive Distortions	Being able to name the *way* you are thinking (e.g., catastrophizing) helps you step outside the thought process that makes unwanted thoughts and urges to respond to them so upsetting. When you understand the cognitive distortions leading to your unwanted thoughts, you can be less fused with them and respond to them more mindfully.
False Project vs. Real Project Modified Automatic Thought Record	Many of the difficulties we have with our unwanted thoughts and related emotions come from trying to be certain about the past or future instead of addressing the challenges right in front of us. By writing out what triggered you and what thinking style can be found in your response, you can also identify a more objective and balanced viewpoint.

Tool	Function
In Vivo ERP	Unwanted intrusive thoughts come in many forms, and in most cases, there's a way to confront them head-on with in vivo ERP. You can start by writing out a hierarchy that represents the challenge level of each exposure, then identify how you will make direct contact with the unwanted thoughts. If the thoughts are about contamination, this may look like touching triggering objects without washing. If the thoughts are about unwanted acts of harm, then in vivo ERP may entail allowing yourself to be near triggering objects without engaging in safety behaviors.
Imaginal ERP	If your unwanted thoughts do not lend themselves to in vivo exposures, or if the fear is more of a story than a simple thought (e.g., a story of getting sick and being a burden on your loved ones), then writing out an exposure narrative can be helpful. Refer to the tips in chapter 3 for how to do this effectively. Your resulting "script" can include a repeated exposure as you work to overcome your unwanted thoughts.
Interoceptive ERP	For unwanted thoughts related to sensations in the body, exposures that affect your physiological state can be useful. For example, if you have a fear of blushing in front of others, you might do exposure to jogging in place before engaging in a social encounter. Or if you have a fear of panic attacks, you might practice spinning in a chair to generate the feeling of dizziness to practice coping with it. Notice that this tool, as an exposure technique, intentionally generates *unwanted* sensations in the body and serves a different function from tools that help you relax or reduce unwanted feelings.
Trigger/ Distress/ Response Log	Identifying and resisting compulsions in the face of unwanted thoughts is a critical skill to master. This log can help you track unwanted thoughts that arise, identify the distress they cause, and clarify the way you are responding in the moment. This tool can be immensely useful in accurately identifying and eliminating the compulsions that may be keeping you stuck.
Hierarchy Builder	If you're not sure where to start when it comes to exposure, you can use this tool to help organize your exposures from easiest to hardest.

DBT Tools and Skills

These strategies are presented in chapter 4, along with their associated practices and exercises.

Tool	Function
Mindfulness Skills	Many of us live on automatic pilot, doing things out of habit. For many of life's tasks, this makes perfect sense, but it's not the way to live when you are suffering with strong emotions. Mindfulness helps you determine if you are acting in emotion mind (mood-dependent behavior), rational mind, (without attending to your emotions), or wise mind (integrating emotions and facts). The specific skills of observing the moment, engaging with it fully, doing so without judgment, and focusing solely on doing what the situation needs are critical in acting in alignment with your long-term goals.
Interpersonal Effectiveness Skills	Because strong emotions can negatively impact your life in many ways, this skill set has three primary goals: • To obtain your objectives: when what you want is reasonable, asking for it clearly and precisely is more likely to lead to goal attainment. • To maintain healthy relationships: when intense emotions have led you to conflict with someone you care about, relationship effectiveness skills can repair and sustain a stronger relationship with them. • To maintain self-respect: if you have a hard time saying no to others and tend to be a doormat in relationships, building your self-respect will allow you to set limits and stick to your values.
Distress Tolerance Skills	These skills are most helpful when you are in distress and don't have an immediate solution to the problem. If you are about to act ineffectively, using the STOP skill is an effective way to proceed mindfully. You can also use the TIPP skill to change or reduce the intensity of your body's physiological response. STOP and TIPP are two of the most powerful distress tolerance skills, but there are others, like distraction, visual imagery, and relaxations techniques. **IMPORTANT NOTE:** When using distress tolerance skills, you want to make sure that you're not using them to avoid the ERP skills needed to deal with intrusive and unwanted thoughts, because avoidance of ERP can lead to the persistence of unwanted thoughts.

Tool	Function
Radical Acceptance	This skill belongs in the distress tolerance module, but it warrants being pulled out on its own because of the essential role it plays for people who wish their reality were different. This skill is about learning how to stop fighting reality, how to stop acting impulsively or destructively when things aren't going the way you want them to, and how to let go of the things keeping you in a state of bitterness. This skill does not deny past events; rather, it accepts that they happened and that there's nothing you can do to go back to them in the present moment. Accepting things as they were and as they are, even when you feel uncomfortable, even when you feel life is unfair, allows you to be the master of your experiences instead of vice versa and frees you from spending a lot of energy fighting reality. Radical acceptance also entails noticing that fighting reality does not change reality.
Emotion Regulation Skills	Intense emotions can lead to a cascade of unhelpful behaviors that can adversely affect you and disrupt your relationships. The emotion regulation skills of DBT teach you to identify your emotions and understand their function, as well as the action urges that typically accompany them. These skills attend to the emotional impact of such vulnerability factors as sleep quality, lack of exercise, drug use, and an unbalanced diet. The tool of opposite action within this skill set teaches you to use behaviors opposite to the ones that keep you in unwanted emotional states.
Coping Ahead	This skill belongs to the emotion regulation cluster, but again, it's worth calling out on its own because you can use it right now! Use this skill when you are worried about some bad outcome of a future event. You imagine that the bad outcome occurs and then rehearse what you would do about it. If you've planned for an unwanted result that doesn't actually happen, then you're all set. But if it does happen, at least you can activate your plan to better cope with the situation.

Final Takeaways

You've taken in a lot of words and concepts. We hope the very title of this book makes clear that unwanted thoughts and intense emotions are part of the human experience, not personal defects or exclusive to the realm of mental illness. We also hope you now recognize that there are multiple tools and combinations of tools to help you when you're burdened by unwanted thoughts and intense emotions. Lastly, we hope you remember that your experience of being you is valid right now, in this moment, even if you can still strengthen your skill set, and that you are worthy of love and respect even when your thoughts and emotions get the better of you. You matter.

For Further Reading

To make it easier for you to navigate this workbook, we intentionally avoided heavy scientific references and citations. But many of our ideas and conclusions rest on the shoulders of previous works in which the concepts and strategies we've presented are explored in one way or another, to a greater or lesser degree. Here's a list of the most seminal resources you may wish to reference to deepen your exploration of the subjects covered in this book.

Abramowitz, J. S., B. J. Deacon, and S. P. H. Whiteside. 2011. *Exposure Therapy for Anxiety: Principles and Practice.* New York: Guilford Press.

Aguirre, B., and G. Galen. 2013. *Mindfulness for Borderline Personality Disorder: Relieve Your Suffering Using the Core Skill of Dialectical Behavior Therapy.* Oakland, CA: New Harbinger Publications.

Baer, L. 2002. *The Imp of the Mind: Exploring the Silent Epidemic of Obsessive Bad Thoughts.* New York: Plume.

Galen, G., and B. Aguirre. 2021. *DBT for Dummies.* Hoboken, NJ: John Wiley & Sons.

Grayson, J. 2014. *Freedom from Obsessive Compulsive Disorder: A Personalized Recovery Program for Living with Uncertainty.* Updated ed. New York: Penguin Group.

Hershfield, J., and S. Nicely. 2017. *Everyday Mindfulness for OCD: Tips, Tricks, and Skills for Living Joyfully.* Oakland, CA: New Harbinger Publications.

Hershfield, J., and T. Corboy. 2021. *The Mindfulness Workbook for OCD: A Guide to Overcoming Obsessions and Compulsions Using Mindfulness and Cognitive Behavioral Therapy.* 2nd ed. Oakland, CA: New Harbinger Publications.

Linehan, M. M. 1993. *Cognitive-Behavioral Treatment of Borderline Personality Disorder.* New York: Guilford Press.

Linehan, M. M. 2015. *DBT Skills Training Manual.* 2nd ed. New York: Guilford Press.

Neff, K. 2011. *Self-Compassion: Stop Beating Yourself Up and Leave Insecurity Behind.* New York: William Morrow.

Jon Hershfield, MFT, is director of The Center for OCD and Anxiety at Sheppard Pratt in Towson, MD. He specializes in the use of mindfulness and cognitive behavioral therapy (CBT) for obsessive-compulsive disorder (OCD) and related disorders. Jon is a member of the Scientific and Clinical Advisory Board of the International OCD Foundation, and is on the faculty of their Behavioral Therapy Training Institute. He is author of *Overcoming Harm OCD*, *When a Family Member Has OCD*, and *The OCD Workbook for Teens*; and coauthor of *The Mindfulness Workbook for OCD* and *Everyday Mindfulness for OCD*.

Blaise Aguirre, MD, is assistant professor of psychiatry at Harvard Medical School, and an expert in child, adolescent, and adult psychotherapy, including dialectical behavior therapy (DBT), He is founding medical director of McLean 3East—a continuum of care using DBT and related techniques to treat complex psychiatric disorders including borderline personality disorder (BPD). Aguirre has been a staff psychiatrist at McLean since 2000, and is internationally recognized for his extensive work in the treatment of mood and personality disorders in adolescents. He lectures regularly in Europe, Africa, and the Middle East on DBT and BPD. Aguirre is author of many books, including *Borderline Personality Disorder in Adolescents* and *Depression* (*Biographies of Disease*); and coauthor of *Mindfulness for Borderline Personality Disorder*, *Coping with BPD*, *DBT for Dummies*, and *Helping Your Troubled Teen*.

FROM OUR COFOUNDER—

As cofounder of New Harbinger and a clinical psychologist since 1978, I know that emotional problems are best helped with evidence-based therapies. These are the treatments derived from scientific research (randomized controlled trials) that show what works. Whether these treatments are delivered by trained clinicians or found in a self-help book, they are designed to provide you with proven strategies to overcome your problem.

Therapies that aren't evidence-based—whether offered by clinicians or in books—are much less likely to help. In fact, therapies that aren't guided by science may not help you at all. That's why this New Harbinger book is based on scientific evidence that the treatment can relieve emotional pain.

This is important: if this book isn't enough, and you need the help of a skilled therapist, use the following resources to find a clinician trained in the evidence-based protocols appropriate for your problem. And if you need more support—a community that understands what you're going through and can show you ways to cope—resources for that are provided below, as well.

Real help is available for the problems you have been struggling with. The skills you can learn from evidence-based therapies will change your life.

Matthew McKay, PhD
Cofounder, New Harbinger Publications

If you need a therapist, the following organization can help you find a therapist trained in dialectical behavior therapy (DBT).

Behavioral Tech, LLC
please visit www.behavioraltech.org and click on Find a DBT Therapist.

If you need a therapist, the following organization can help you find a therapist trained in cognitive behavioral therapy (CBT).

The Association for Behavioral & Cognitive Therapies (ABCT) Find-a-Therapist service offers a list of therapists schooled in CBT techniques. Therapists listed are licensed professionals who have met the membership requirements of ABCT and who have chosen to appear in the directory.
Please visit www.abct.org and click on Find a Therapist.

For additional support for patients, family, and friends, please contact the following:

Depression and Bipolar Support Alliance (DBSA) **visit www.dbsalliance.org**

National Center for PTSD **visit www.ptsd.va.gov**

BPD Central **visit www.bpdcentral.org**

International OCD Foundation (IOCDF) **visit www.ocfoundation.org**

National Suicide Prevention Lifeline
Call 24 hours a day 1-800-273-TALK (8255) or visit www.suicidepreventionlifeline.org

MORE BOOKS from
NEW HARBINGER PUBLICATIONS

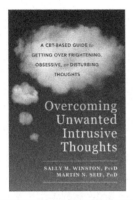

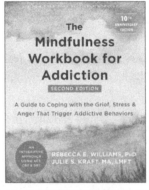
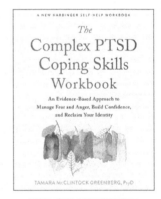